WANNA BET?

Also by Don Wade

Take Dead Aim (a novel)

The PGA Manual of Golf (with Rick Martino)

Talking on Tour

"And Then Justin Told Sergio . . ."

"And Then the Shark Told Justin . . ."

"And Then Tiger Told the Shark . . ."

The Players Championship

"And Then Freddie Told Tiger . . ."

"And Then Seve Told Freddie . . ."

"And Then Fuzzy Told Seve . . ."

Better Golf the Sam Snead Way (with Sam Snead)

"And Then Chi Chi Told Fuzzy . . ."

Ken Venturi's New Stroke Savers (with Ken Venturi)

"And Then Arnie Told Chi Chi . . ."

"And Then Jack Said to Arnie . . ."

Swing Thoughts

Nancy Lopez's The Complete Golfer (with Nancy Lopez)

Amy Alcott's Guide to Women's Golf (with Amy Alcott)

Caddies

WANNA BET?

The Greatest True Stories About Gambling on Golf,
from Titanic Thompson to Tiger Woods

DON WADE

THUNDER'S MOUTH PRESS
NEW YORK

WANNA BET?
The Greatest True Stories About Gambling on Golf,
from Titanic Thompson to Tiger Woods

AVALON
publishing group incorporated

Published by
Thunder's Mouth Press
An Imprint of Avalon Publishing Group
245 West 17th Street, 11th Floor
New York, NY 10011

First printing November 2005

Library of Congress Cataloging-in-Publication Data is available.

ISBN: 1-56025-705-9
ISBN 13: 978-1-56025-705-9

9 8 7 6 5 4 3 2 1

Book design by Maria E. Torres

Printed in the United States

Distributed by Publishers Group West

To my dad—

The mayor of West Concord,
The King of Scrambles,
A great role model,
And an even better man

Thanks, Dad. This one's for you.

CONTENTS

ACKNOWLEDGMENTS

Over the years, I've come to appreciate just how much writing a book is a collaborative effort. For that reason, I want to thank some important people who helped make this book possible.

First, thanks to my editor at Avalon Publishing Group, Jofie Ferrari-Adler. This book was his idea and he's been a delight to work with—patient, supportive, and good-natured. I hope this is just the first of many books we do together.

Next up is Tara Mark, who handled this project as my agent at RLR. She, too, has been a wealth of encouragement and good advice when it comes to navigating the murky waters of publishing. Both she and her advice are much appreciated.

Then there is my old friend Paul Szep, who did the

illustrations. He and I go back a long way and I have admired his work since his first years at the *Boston Globe*, where he won two Pulitzers for his brilliance in comforting the afflicted and afflicting the comfortable. Now, if he could just find one good golf swing and stick with it . . . Thanks, Szeppy.

Then there are all my friends, who contributed so many stories and so much support.

Finally, thanks to Julia, Ben, Darcy, and Andy for their understanding, help, and love. No one could ask for more.

PREFACE

By a happy accident of both birth and fate, I have been around the game of golf virtually all my life.

My mother had two brothers who were golf professionals and a third brother who sold golf equipment for MacGregor. As a result, there were always clubs and balls around the house.

I grew up in Concord, Massachusetts, in a house that was just down the road from the Concord Country Club, a wonderful old club that dates back to the 1800s. Concord is the birthplace of democracy in America. I think Concord Country Club is probably the birthplace of the "nickel nassau." Everything I know and believe about golf gambling is rooted in my many happy years at Concord.

I started caddying when I was twelve years old. The

very first person I caddied for was a delightful old Yankee named Hope Chase. Mrs. Chase was a warm and funny woman and a very good player. However, on my first hole as a caddie, Mrs. Chase knocked her second shot into some thick grass bordering a pond, and, despite our best efforts, it was lost. I felt terrible and volunteered to buy her a new ball after the round.

"Don't worry about it, dear," she said. "I win more of these damned things than I can ever lose."

There were a lot of characters at Concord. One of my favorites was an old codger named Jack Codding, who had an uncanny knack for making holes-in-one. At that time, the company that distributed Drambuie—a Scottish liqueur that, when combined with Scotch whisky, produces the world's greatest cold-weather drink, a Rusty Nail—sponsored a sweepstakes. If you made a hole-in-one, you were eligible to enter. First prize was an all-expenses-paid trip to play the classic courses of Scotland.

Well, as luck would have it, Jack Codding won . . . but there was a hitch. If he accepted, the United States Golf Association would revoke his amateur status. As I recall, Mr. Codding thought it over, decided his chances of ever winning a tournament requiring that he be a certifiable amateur were nil, took the trip, and had a marvelous time.

When I look back on that time, I remember the caddie days, when we'd come to the course on Monday mornings and play all day for free. We'd have all sorts of little bets—greenies, sandies, barkies, Hogans, and Palmers. It seemed like every week somebody would come up with a new game or a new twist on an old one. I also remember that during the club championship, we'd bet on our favorite players. Mine was a guy named Bill O'Brien, a former Marine who looked like John Wayne, had a swing like Sam Snead's, and smoked Lucky Strikes that he lit with a Zippo. After he left the Marines, he became a banker, but I don't think his heart was ever really in it. His heart was in golf.

My first real introduction to the intricacies of gambling came in my senior year of high school, when I was working as an assistant in the golf shop. Johnny Devlin, who also worked in the shop, was a few years older than me and a very fine player. He went to the University of Florida at a time in Concord when going south to college meant going to Yale.

At any rate, that summer he arrived at the club with a brand-new set of Spalding Elite irons, which were beautiful clubs. As I looked at them, I noticed that the 6-iron seemed to have less loft than the 5-iron. In fact, the more I studied the irons, the more I was convinced that the lofts were all screwed up. When I mentioned this to Johnny, he just smiled. It turned out that when he'd ordered the clubs, he had Spalding deliberately mismark some of the numbers on the soles of the irons—the better to throw off any opponent who foolishly tried to go to school on his club selection.

This gambling business was tricky stuff, I was discovering.

In 1978, I went to work as an editor at *Golf Digest* and, happily, the first story I ever did was with Sam Snead. We struck up a wonderful friendship and I wound up working on all his stories for the magazine, as well as coauthoring a book with the Slammer. Along the way, we played a lot of golf and I heard a lot of stories. I developed the same sort of relationship with Amy Alcott, Tom Kite, and many others who I count as friends.

At that time, *Golf Digest* used to hold what were called "Pro Panel" meetings. These were usually three-day sessions attended by some of the greatest teachers in the game—Sam, Dr. Cary "Doc" Middlecoff, Paul Runyan, Bob Toski, Davis Love, Jr., Jim Flick, Peter Kostis, Chuck Cook, Jack Lumpkin, John Elliott, Dr. Bob Rotella, and many others. They were wonderful occasions, not least because of the stories that were told.

Many of them are in this book. I hope you enjoy them.

—Don Wade

WANNA BET?

AMY ALCOTT

A my Alcott won twenty-nine LPGA tournaments, including five majors, and was inducted into the World Golf Hall of Fame in 1999. Beyond her obvious playing ability, her personality and sense of humor made her one of the most popular players in golf.

"The Kid," as she's nicknamed, grew up in Los Angeles and still lives there, dividing her golf between Riviera Country Club and Bel-Air Country Club—one of the best possible doubles in the game.

At Bel-Air, she has a group of friends who play together regularly.

"Jerry West was part of our regular group," said Alcott. "We'd each put $100 in for the medal match and then there'd be team matches and all kinds of junk bets. I play at scratch and most of the other guys are

single-digit handicappers. This one day, we came to the eighteenth tee and Jerry—who is a good player—had a three-stroke lead on me. Basically, I didn't think there was any way he could lose. But then his drive went dead right, hit a tree, and dropped straight down in front of the tee. He decided to play up the first fairway, but his second shot hit a tree. He tried to play his third shot over the trees, but it didn't make it. He tried to punch it onto the green, but he hit it into a green-side bunker. He left his next shot in the bunker and then hit his sixth shot about a foot and a half from the hole. I made a four, but I figured there was no way he was going to miss his putt. Wrong. As soon as the ball went past the hole, his putter was airborne.

" 'That's why they called you "Mr. Clutch," ' one of the players said, and everyone picked up on it.

"Jerry eventually paid up, but it took him a while to come out of the locker room," Amy said.

TOMMY ARMOUR

Tommy Armour was a stern Scot who won a British Open, a U.S. Open, and a PGA Championship. When his playing career was over, he became one of the game's most sought-after teaching professionals.

Armour was one hard character. During World War I, he single-handedly captured a German tank and then, when the tank's commander refused to surrender, he killed the soldier with his bare hands. Years later, when told that players were required to wear numbers pinned to their shirts in order to play in George S. May's World Championship of Golf (the most lucrative tournament of the time), he refused.

"The last time I wore a number was in a German prisoner of war camp," he said, grimly. "I'll never wear another."

This isn't to say Armour didn't have a fine sense of humor—or at least an appreciation for the absurd.

One year he was teamed with Cyril Walker in the Mid-South Open. Now Walker was a strong player, good enough to win the 1924 U.S. Open at Oakland Hills. But he was also a player who was wound up pretty tight.

At any rate, they came to the final hole of an early round and needed a par to stay in the competition. Armour bunkered his approach shot and, after failing to get his next shot onto the putting surface, picked up.

This put all the pressure on Walker, who needed to two-putt from thirty feet. Walker positioned himself to putt, and then bent over to brush a fly off his ball. In the process, he lost his balance and swept his ball off the green. Armour tried to contain himself, but it was impossible. He burst into laughter, which further inflamed an already overwrought Walker, who proceeded to make a seven—which sent them packing.

...

Tommy Armour was paired with Johnny Revolta, a fine player who went on to enjoy a reputation as a respected teacher, in a tournament in California in the 1930s.

Revolta was near the lead in the closing stretch of holes in the final round when he left a four-footer short of the hole.

"Gutless," yelled a man in the gallery.

Armour wheeled around and walked over to the crowd, where he pointed to the man and issued a challenge.

"I'll bet you any amount of money you can't make that same putt," said Armour.

"Don't be ridiculous," said the man.

They agreed that the man would face the identical putt right after the close of the tournament. The bet was $5,000, which Armour raised from his fellow professionals.

A ball was placed in the exact spot and a large crowd gathered around the green. A hush fell as the man addressed the ball. He began sweating profusely and his hands started to tremble. Finally, he backed away and tried to steady himself. When he finally hit the putt, the ball came to rest well short and wide of the hole.

"I want to apologize to Mr. Revolta," the man said. "When I got over the ball I couldn't even see the hole. I had no idea what the pressure could do to you."

"In that case," said Armour, "pick up your money. The bet is off."

SEVE BALLESTEROS

In his prime, Spain's Seve Ballesteros was simply a genius. He won three British Opens and two Masters and there was never anyone more compelling to watch. He could hit shots under pressure that other players could only dream about hitting. In fact, he had shots that most players couldn't even imagine.

When it came to shot-making, however, he did have one equal, and that was Lee Trevino. Both believed they were unbeatable in a one-club competition, and a match was arranged between the two players on the Old Course at St. Andrews, the day after the 1984 British Open—a contest, by the way, that Ballesteros won. The match was televised by the BBC.

The two agreed to a nine-hole match, though the

holes would be nonconsecutive because of construction on the course. They would both use 5-irons.

Playing the 175-yard par-3 eleventh as their opening hole, Ballesteros got up and down from the Strath bunker—no small accomplishment with fourteen clubs to choose from, let alone with only a 5-iron.

When the players returned to the eleventh hole, the TV guys asked Seve to replicate his shot. When he did, and came up just a bit short, Trevino scooped up the ball with his cap.

In the end, however, the Old Course proved to be the wrong place for such a competition. The conditions were just too difficult. Trevino wound up four-putting number two and shot a 40, while Ballesteros was only slightly better, shooting a 38.

AL BESSELINK

A l Besselink played on the PGA Tour in the 1950s and 1960s, and while he enjoyed only modest success, it's fair to say that he had more than his share of good times. Even though he never had a lot of money, he never seemed to worry about it because he knew he had enough skill—and luck—to get by.

"Bessie was one of the nicest guys in the world," recalled the late Dave Marr, who won the 1965 PGA Championship and was a friend of Besselink's. "Everybody wanted to help him out, but you knew if you loaned him money you could color it missing in action. And he was generous with his money. The problem was, he just didn't have that much that often."

Marr recalled the time Besselink was supposed to

travel to South America for a tournament but didn't have enough money to get there.

"Bessie figured he'd go to a racetrack in Miami and try to win enough to get to the tournament," Marr said. "He lost everything. He was completely tapped out. On his way out of the track, he kicked over a ticket and, sure enough, it was a winner. That could only happen to Bessie. He won enough to get to the tournament and won enough money at the tournament to get to Las Vegas, where the first Tournament of Champions was being played. He was playing pretty well, but no one knew it because the news from South America never made it to the American papers. When he got to Las Vegas, he checked the odds on the field and found out he was probably the longest shot in the tournament. He bet everything he had on himself, won the tournament, and cleaned up on the bet. In those days, first prize was $10,000 in silver dollars, so Bessie was in heaven.

"Typical of Bessie, though," continued Marr, "he gave most of the money to the Damon Runyon Cancer Fund and never made a big deal about it. Most people didn't hear about it until years later."

TOMMY BOLT

Tommy Bolt, a member of the World Golf Hall of Fame, is one of the greatest shot-makers—and characters—in the history of the game. His victory in the 1958 U.S. Open served as validation of his enormous talent.

Bolt was known for his temper and for his willingness to give good quotes to writers who covered the tour. He was also the subject of great stories: like the time he laid down the greatest challenge of his career.

One day, after missing another short putt, he threw down his putter and looked toward the sky.

"You did it to me again, didn't you, God?" he said. "Why don't you come down here and we'll play. And bring that boy of yours, too. I'll play your best ball."

...

Tommy Bolt used to augment his tour winnings by playing high-stakes betting matches. He particularly favored Hot Springs, Arkansas, where he could regularly fleece one of his favorite marks, a Mr. Louis Marrow. According to Bolt, Mr. Marrow was perfect in almost every possible way.

"He owned a chain of successful furniture stores, had a big bank account, a fast backswing, and a drinking problem," Bolt recalled. "He'd come to Hot Springs to take the cure and try and dry out. He loved to play but he couldn't hit the ground with his hat. We'd play $1,500 nassaus. I'd give him a million strokes, but it didn't matter. The last time we played, he came to the last hole and, by some miracle, had a two-footer to win. I was getting a little nervous, you see, but it really didn't matter. Old Louis got the shakes so bad the putter fell out of his hands. He didn't have a prayer. It was the easiest money I ever made."

THE BOYS

The Boys are a group of my friends who are passionate golfers from the Connecticut–New York area, but truth be told, you can find guys like the Boys at any club in any part of the country.

This story may be apocryphal—in fact, it probably is, since I've heard so many variations of it over the years. Still, it's worth telling.

Two men—who'd never particularly liked each other—met in the finals of the club championship. It was a close match, and on one of the final holes, both players hooked their drives into the woods.

One man found a ball and motioned his opponent over to examine the situation.

"Is this ground under repair?" he asked his opponent.

"No," the man said.

"OK, then is this casual water?" the first man asked.

"No, not even close," said his opponent.

"Well, then can I get line-of-sight relief?" he asked.

"No, of course not," his opponent said.

"So you're absolutely sure the ball has to be played as it lies?" the first man said.

"Yes, you know the rules as well as I do," his opponent said.

"Good," said the first man. "It's your ball. Good luck."

...

Until his retirement in 2005, my friend Bill Repko was one of the nation's top "workout banking" specialists, which basically meant that the crummier the economy got, the busier he became.

One pleasant part of his job was playing in outings his bank held for bankruptcy lawyers and judges. These were played at some wonderful venues, including the Kittansett Club in Massachusetts, Torrey Pines, and Spyglass Hill—to name just three.

The year the outing was held at Spyglass Hill, Bill's group had a healthy little match going on the side.

When they came to the seventeenth hole, the match was very tight and time was running out. The seventeenth at Spyglass Hill is a short, dogleg left par-4. Bill hit a perfect drive, setting up an easy approach to the green.

"That's where Grandma hides the cookies," his caddie said.

The foursome broke up.

"What does that mean?" Bill asked the caddie.

"It means you found the sweet spot."

...

Two of my friends, Tim Cassidy and Dennis Powell, play a lot of golf together. Occasionally, the bets get a little complicated.

"We played one day and when we made the turn, Dennis let us know where all the bets stood," recalled Cassidy. "There was the nassau on the front nine, the presses, the greenies, sandies, Palmers, Watsons, Hogans, and all the rest. When he finished, I asked him what everyone shot."

"I don't know," Dennis said. "I didn't have room on the scorecard to keep the scores."

HARRY BRADSHAW

Ireland's Harry Bradshaw was a gifted player with a wonderful short game who teamed with fellow countryman Christy O'Connor to win the 1958 World Cup against many of the best players in the world.

Bradshaw loved Ireland and never felt the need to travel around the world to play golf. As a result, most people never fully appreciated what a beautiful player he really was.

In 1971, he was pitted against Billy Casper in a match at Bradshaw's home course, Portmarnock. Dublin's bookies put the odds at 7-1 in Casper's favor, which came as no surprise to Bradshaw.

"I can understand the boys' thinking," Bradshaw said. "Casper would beat me anyplace else in the world, and easily enough, but at Portmarnock? If I were a betting man I might wager a pound or two on myself."

That was all the locals needed to hear. They raced to the bookmakers to get bets down on Bradshaw before the odds dropped. Sure enough, Bradshaw neatly dusted Casper and the locals won more than enough to raise a pint or two in honor of Dear Old Harry.

MARK CALCAVECCHIA

Mark Calcavecchia won the 1989 British Open in a playoff with two Australians, Greg Norman and Wayne Grady. It was the first time the Royal and Ancient Golf Club of St. Andrews had settled the championship via a four-hole, cumulative medal score instead of the traditional eighteen-hole playoff. It was fitting that Calcavecchia won in a playoff, since he loves the pressure of head-to-head competition—often with a little something riding on the outcome.

"One of my most memorable matches was against Phil Mickelson during a practice round for the British Open," Calcavecchia recalled. "We had a regular bet going and we also had a $1,000 bet that you'd win if you shot 66 or better. Phil made ten-footers on fifteen, six-teen, and seventeen and shot a 66. I promise you, he was grinding on those putts like it was the final round of a major championship."

...

For many years, one of Mark Calcavecchia's favorite partners in practice-round matches was Ken Green. One year at THE PLAYERS Championship, Calcavecchia and Green faced off against Paul Azinger and Blaine McCallister. The match was close until the final stretch of holes when Azinger and McCallister went birdie, birdie, eagle, birdie, birdie to run the table and collect $2,500.

"The worst part was that Blaine chipped in on the last hole to really stick it to us," said Green.

CALCUTTAS

In the early years of the Masters, the calcutta was one of the highlights of the week. People would bet—and often considerable amounts—on their favorites. As the week progressed and players either missed the cut or moved up or down the leaderboard, fans would buy shares of a player or a group of players.

In 1946, Herman Keiser attended the calcutta party and, seeing that the odds on his winning were 20-1, pried open his wallet and—he was not a man to part with his money lightly—sprang for $20.

Keiser was a good player, and he went out and shot rounds of 68-69 to take a five-stroke lead over Ben Hogan into the weekend. Not surprisingly, Hogan had been one of the pretournament favorites and was attracting a lot of bets. As the weekend arrived, people were scrambling to get additional bets down on him. One member reportedly put down an additional $40,000 on Hogan.

Keiser was approached by two members of the calcutta committee, who asked if he'd like to increase his bet on himself. Keiser thought about it for a moment and asked if he could get $50 down at the pretournament odds.

"I told them that if I couldn't hold onto a five-stroke lead, then I didn't deserve to win, against Ben or anyone else," he said.

In the final round, Keiser was paired with Byron Nelson, a true sportsman and one of the best players you could possibly hope to play with under the pressure of the final round of a major championship. In those days, players weren't necessarily paired according to score, but more or less based on the whims of tournament officials. In this case, Hogan was paired with Jimmy Demaret in the final group of the day, while Keiser and Nelson had an earlier starting time.

Keiser played well and when he came to the final hole, hit his approach thirty feet from the flag.

"Herman, do you realize you haven't three-putted once this week?" said Nelson, trying to give Keiser a little boost of confidence.

"Yes, but I still have some work left here," said Keiser.

Three putts later he was in the clubhouse and Nelson was a mess.

"Poor Byron was sure he'd jinxed me," said Keiser. "He felt horrible. He must have apologized a dozen times."

Sitting with his friend Henry Picard, the winner of the 1938 Masters, as he waited for Hogan to complete his round, Keiser was a nervous wreck.

"C'mon, Herman," said Picard, "let's go out and see how Ben finishes."

"No, you go and then come back and tell me how he did," said Keiser.

After what must have seemed an eternity, Picard returned.

"Ben made a heck of a putt . . ." Picard happily reported, ". . . for a five."

For his efforts, Keiser took home the $1,500 winner's prize plus a nice bonus from the calcutta pool.

And for his part, Byron Nelson left Augusta a much-relieved man.

...

In 1938, Byron Nelson agreed to attend the pretournament calcutta at the Masters as a favor to club officials, who thought that having the defending champion in attendance might be a nice touch. Nelson didn't really much approve of gambling, but he made an appearance, said a few words, and then repaired to the back of the room.

Bidding began at $100, but when Ben Hogan's name was called, the room fell silent. Feeling badly for his boyhood friend (the two got their start in golf as caddies), Nelson bought Hogan for $100.

"The next day, Ben asked if he could buy half of himself and I said that would be fine," said Nelson. "It took Ben some time to scrape the $50 together, but he did. Ben finished twenty-fifth and out of the money, but I always thought that gave him a little bit of confidence."

...

Deepdale Golf Club is one of the most exclusive clubs in the metropolitan New York area and has been for a long time. The club was famous for its big calcutta tournament, which annually attracted top players and hefty betters from up and down the East Coast. Since it was a private affair, no one much worried about it—until a scandal rocked the club in 1955 and forced the

United States Golf Association to act on large-scale gambling.

The scandal began when a low-handicap amateur somehow received one of the treasured invitations—which had been meant for another player. He and another low-handicapper entered, claiming to have considerably higher handicaps than they really did. For whatever reason, tournament officials neglected to check either man's identity or handicap. The team went on to shoot rounds of 58-57, which won its flight and the $45,000 pool.

Not surprisingly, club officials began to look into the men's backgrounds, and soon the story made its way into the New York press. Under growing pressure, one of the men confessed, apologizing to both the club and the other players, and also to the original invitee.

Ultimately, he returned his share of the winnings. His partner and a third conspirator, however, refused to return their share of the payout. In addition, Deepdale members who had purchased a share of the team elected to donate their winnings to charity.

In the end, the USGA used the scandal to put an end to large-scale calcuttas like those at Deepdale.

Several years after the Deepdale Calcutta scandal, the Golf Writers Association of America invited Joseph C. Dey, the executive director of the United States Golf Association, to participate in its annual golf outing in Myrtle Beach.

Now, to put this in its proper perspective, Dey was a man of great personal rectitude, and the golf writers' tournament was an often-raucous affair comprised of equal parts golf and drinking. It also included a calcutta, which was a problem.

As Bob Drum, the colorful (to put it mildly) president of the organization, began the calcutta's auction, Dey voiced his concerns to the Drummer.

"Bob, this isn't a calcutta, is it?" Dey asked.

"Not at all, Joe," said Drum, thinking quickly. "We call it a Bombay."

…

One year in the early 1980s, Bob Drum was playing in the golf writers' tournament, which was held on the eve of the Masters. Naturally, he had some pretty healthy bets going with his playing partners and, almost as naturally, he managed to lose them all.

When he returned to the clubhouse, there was a message ordering him to come to the Augusta National Golf Club immediately. The message was from Frank Chirkinian, the executive producer and director of golf coverage at CBS Sports and the man who had given the Drummer the only job that ever paid him any decent money.

Drummer immediately made plans to leave for Augusta. The only problem was that his opponents— not willing to take a chance on Drum leaving town without settling his bets—had taken his golf clubs hostage and locked them in their car.

Drum tried to reason with the writers, promising to pay them when they got to the Masters. Having heard that before, they weren't buying it, so Drummer did the only logical thing: he grabbed an iron from a nearby bag and smashed in one of the car windows, liberating his bag and freeing him to flee to Augusta.

WINSTON CHURCHILL

Britain's greatest prime minister is famously credited with describing golf as "a game whose aim is to put a very small ball in a very small hole with weapons singularly ill-designed for the purpose," which he may or may not have thought up—or even said, but never mind.

To the extent that Churchill dabbled in golf, it was largely for social—which is to say, political—purposes. Before he became prime minister, he, along with twenty-four other members of Parliament, was a member of Walton Heath, the exclusive club outside London.

As luck would have it, one day he was playing with David Lloyd George, who was then prime minister. On the final green, Churchill faced a putt for the match— but then, playfully, decided to raise the stakes.

"I shall now putt you for the prime minister's office," he said.

He missed, but would mercifully become prime minister soon enough.

BILL CLINTON

Whatever Bill Clinton might lack in golfing ability, he more than makes up for with his sheer enthusiasm for the game. While some people criticized him for his generous use of mulligans or takeovers—or Billigans, as they came to be known—few could find fault with his love of the camaraderie that is so much a part of golf.

One time President Clinton traveled to Ireland and wisely set aside some time in his schedule for a round of golf with Christy O'Connor at Ballybunion, one of the world's most spectacular courses. He even managed to make a little money while he was there.

"When I got to the course, they asked me what my handicap was," Clinton recalled. "At the time I was playing pretty good, so I told them I was about a twelve.

They asked me if I'd played many links courses. I told them I had only played two. They bet me 20-1 odds that I couldn't break 100. After I made a seven on the first hole, I was beginning to think they might be right. But I actually got a good feel for the course and after fifteen holes I was only ten over par, which was pretty good because the wind was just howling. I fell apart on the last three holes but I still shot a 95. I'm pretty proud of that round."

...

Another time, Clinton was playing with Hawaii governor John Waihee when he received a lesson in the importance of home-course advantage.

"We were playing a course on the Big Island and, instead of sand in the bunkers, there was ground-up lava," Clinton explained. "There was all this lava off to the sides of the holes, too. I had a blind second shot and John told me to hit it a little bit to the right of the center of the fairway. I hit it and it kind of drifted off. When we came over the rise, I could see my ball was in the lava.

" 'Why didn't you tell me there was lava over there?' I asked him.

" 'You didn't ask me,' he said.

"So we're playing along and he starts to tell me how he's a direct descendant of King Kamehameha, who unified the Hawaiian Islands, and that the natives really believe in ancestor guardians that look after true believers. Then he hits his shot right into the same lava where I hit mine, except his bounces off the lava and ends up right back in the fairway.

" 'See, I told you,' he said.

" 'Where do I sign up?' I asked."

FRED COUPLES

F red Couples, the winner of the 1992 Masters, is easily one of the most popular players on the PGA Tour—in no small part thanks to his easygoing personality and seemingly effortless approach to the game.

Unlike many modern players, who learned the game at private clubs, Couples learned to play on a public course in Seattle, where his father worked for the parks and recreation department.

"My family wasn't rich by any means, but every day in the summer my parents would give me $5 and send me off to the golf course," Couples recalled. "That was a lot of money for a kid in those days. It cost me $3.50 to play all day and I could buy a hamburger and a Coke for a buck and a half.

"The funny thing was, I almost never played with

kids my own age. I was always playing against older guys who were, like, in their fifties and sixties and it was a blast. We'd have small bets, but it was mostly just fun being out there and competing against those guys. Some of them were pretty good players, too.

"What I really liked were the skins games we'd play on the par-three course. We'd play a dime a skin and there'd be ten or fifteen guys playing, and if you won a few skins you'd go home with a ton of dimes. That's when golf was really fun."

BING CROSBY

Bing Crosby was an excellent golfer, skilled enough to play in both the British and the United States Amateurs. Naturally he attracted large galleries at both.

When living in Los Angeles, Crosby played most of his golf at the Lakeside Golf Club. One day he lost a close match to a hustler named John "Mysterious" Montague. Crosby hated to lose, and even though he was quite wealthy, he hated paying off his bets even more than hated losing—a fact not lost on Montague.

"Bing," he said. "I can handle you with a shovel, a bat, and a rake."

Crosby couldn't help himself. He agreed to play one hole, double or nothing, for the amount he had already lost.

They went to the first hole, where Crosby hit the green in two and two-putted for his par.

Montague hit the ball with the bat twice, his second shot coming to rest in a green-side bunker. He managed to scrape it out onto the green with the shovel, and then, using the rake like a pool cue, ran in the putt to tie Crosby.

Crosby who had seen enough, shook his head and went straight to the clubhouse for a good, stiff drink. He had seen all he wanted to see of Mysterious Montague.

...

Although he was a very wealthy man, both from his show business career and from some very shrewd investments, Bing and his money were rarely parted in haste.

On one occasion, Bing and Byron Nelson lost a match to Bob Hope and Jimmy Demaret. Crosby wasn't carrying any cash but promised he'd pay Hope later.

Some time passed and the bet was never settled. One day, Hope happened to walk into the pro shop at Lakeside Country Club, where he and Crosby were both members. Crosby had just made a purchase and his change was on the counter. Hope sprang into action, swiping a $20 bill from Crosby's change and racing out the door. The resulting foot race was like something out of their "*Road to . . .*" movies.

BERNARD DARWIN

Bernard Darwin was the legendary golf correspondent for the *Times* of London and a player skilled enough to play for the Great Britain/Ireland team in the first Walker Cup matches, which were played at the National Golf Links in 1922.

Darwin was so influential that no less a player than Harry Vardon once said, "I never know how well I played until I read Mr. Darwin's verdict in the next day's *Times*."

But as legendary as Darwin was for his insightful writing, he was nearly as well known for his volcanic temper on the golf course.

One day he was playing a friendly match involving a healthy wager. Like many—indeed most—of the players of that era preceding Gene Sarazen's invention of the sand wedge, he struggled mightily to escape from bunkers, although Darwin was said to struggle harder than most. As the match reached the closing hole, Darwin bunkered his approach shot, failed to escape, and subsequently lost the match. After his final failed attempt from the hazard, he let loose a string of expletives that demonstrated, if nothing else, the depth and breadth of his vocabulary. Finally, he concluded by looking toward the heavens and beseeching the Lord to come to his aid, adding, "And don't send your son, either. This is man's work!"

...

On another occasion, Darwin felt so put upon that he fell to his knees, bit out a clump of turf, and, after spitting it out, shouted, "Oh, God, now are you satisfied? Have you humiliated me enough for one day?"

LEO DIEGEL

Leo Diegel was a brilliant player who won the PGA Championship in 1928 and 1929. Unfortunately, he played at a time when golf was dominated by Bobby Jones and Walter Hagen, so he didn't win as many tournaments as he might have in another era.

Diegel had a favorite hustle that he used to pull on unsuspecting pigeons. He'd offer to play the front nine hitting shots while standing on just his right foot, and then play the back nine standing on just his left.

If all that wasn't enough, he had another trick that never failed: he'd offer them a chance to win their money back—double-or-nothing—on a third nine that he'd play hitting shots with his legs crossed.

DWIGHT D. EISENHOWER

President Dwight D. Eisenhower loved golf and wasn't opposed to the occasional bet on his matches. One day he teamed with Bob Hope in a match against General Omar Bradley and Senator Stuart Symington at Burning Tree Country Club outside Washington. Hope played poorly and the team lost $4 each. The next day Eisenhower and Bradley teamed in a match against Hope and Senator Prescott Bush, the grandfather of President George W. Bush. Hope played very well, shooting a 74.

"Why didn't you play like that yesterday?" Eisenhower asked as he reluctantly paid Hope.

...

One time President Eisenhower was playing a match with some friends at Burning Tree, which used to give presidents honorary memberships until President Jimmy Carter, in a fit of morality, decided it was unbecoming for a president to play golf at a private club when he could be out fishing for bass among the masses or some such thing.

Now, as anyone who has played much golf knows, it's not unusual for the caddies to have bets down on the player they're caddying for, and this day was no exception. Unfortunately for his caddie, Ike wasn't at the top of his game that day, and the caddie decided to step in and give the president some advice.

"You gots to slow it down, baldy," the caddie said. "We gonna get killed if you don't slow it down, boss."

One of the other golfers took the caddie aside and told him that he had to show more respect when speaking to the president—if he had to speak at all.

The next time Ike hit a good shot, the caddie was properly deferential.

"Good shot, President Lincoln," said the caddie.

JOE EZAR

Joe Ezar was a brilliant trick-shot artist, as talented as the legendary Joe Kirkwood or any of the others who plied their trade over the years. His greatest performance, however, was easily the one he pulled off during a 1936 exhibition tour through Europe with England's Henry Cotton, who would win three British Opens in the course of his career.

When they arrived in Sestriere, Italy, their host, the president of Fiat, met them for lunch. Ezar bet the man that he could tie—not beat, but tie—the course record the following day. The man agreed to pay 5,000 lira if Ezar shot a 66—but he would pay 10,000 lira for a 65 and a whopping 40,000 lira for a 64.

Ezar took the bet one step further.

"Not only will I take that bet, but I'll write down exactly what score I'll shoot on every hole," Ezar said.

The only problem with Ezar's schedule for this particular exhibition was that it left him with plenty of time on his hands, which generally meant seeking out a local bar or restaurant and happily whiling away the hours. This is just what he did for the rest of the afternoon and a large chunk of the evening.

The next morning he arrived on the first tee looking very much the worse for wear. Still, 40,000 was a lot of lira and Ezar went to work—albeit slowly. He matched his predicted scores on the first eight holes, made a four instead of a three on number nine, but followed that with a three instead of a four on the tenth. From there on it was smooth sailing—he matched each of his predictions and happily left Sestriere with his pockets lined with liras.

BRAD FAXON

B rad Faxon learned the game as a kid growing up in
Rhode Island and joined the tour in 1983 after a
brilliant amateur career. In the years that followed, he
has enjoyed a fine career, in no small part because he is
one of the greatest putters the game has ever seen.

"One year at the British Open, Tom Watson introduced me to a game called 'thousand-dollar no-bogeys,'"
Faxon recalled. "The idea is that if you can go eighteen
holes without making a bogey and the guys you're
playing with can't, each player has to pay you $1,000. I
was playing a practice round with Corey Pavin, Ben
Crenshaw, and Davis Love at the 1994 British Open at
Turnberry. It was just an absolutely beautiful day and we
decided to play Watson's game. Ben bogeyed the second
hole, Davis bogeyed the twelfth and Corey bogeyed the

fourteenth. The last four holes might be the most fun I've ever had on a golf course. Those guys were all over me. It was brutal and unbelievably funny. After I hit my drive on eighteen, I offered them a $975 buyout but there were no takers. I made my par and everyone paid me $1,000. It took a little while, but I finally got a check from the last guy. It was great . . . but I'll tell you that at least one wife wasn't happy when she found out about it."

DICK FISHER

The late Dick Fisher was the chairman and CEO of Morgan Stanley and one of the most respected people in the financial world. Although he'd been stricken with polio as a youngster, he was a passionate golfer who loved playing despite the results of polio.

"The best round I ever played was at Augusta National, with Warren Anderson, then the president of Union Carbide; Rawleigh Warner, the CEO of Mobil; and Ward Foshay, who was on the executive committee of the United States Golf Association," Fisher once recalled. "I was an eighteen handicapper at the time, two higher than my lowest handicap.

"We started on the back nine, and I bogeyed the tenth hole, which was a triumph for me. I made pars on the eleventh and twelfth holes and then birdied the par-five thirteenth. Standing on the eighteenth tee, I was four over par and Rawleigh and I were five-up. The caddies bet on every hole and they settled on the way to the next tee. I think my caddie decided that my cane must have been part of a hustle, but he was making money and he wasn't taking any chances. I hit my drive into the woods on eighteen and by the time I got to my ball, the lie was perfect. I hit a three-iron up near the green and then chipped in for a 3-over-par 39. I was in heaven. Foshay's caddie came up to me and asked me what my handicap was.

" 'Eighteen,' I said.

" 'You ought to be arrested,' he said."

WHITEY FORD

Whitey Ford was a brilliant pitcher for the New York Yankees during their glory years in the 1950s and 1960s. He was later voted into the Baseball Hall of Fame.

Whitey Ford and Mickey Mantle were the closest of friends—a friendship that extended off the playing field and long after their playing days were over.

"One year Mickey and I were playing in the All-Star game in San Francisco," Ford recalled. "On the day before the game, Horace Stoneham, the owner of the San Francisco Giants, invited us to play golf at the Olympic Club. He told us to sign his name for everything—so we did. We signed for the golf, the caddies, golf shoes, sweaters, lunch, drinks—everything. The total came to about $800, and we felt bad about it and decided to tell him.

"He offered to go double-or-nothing on the $800 if I could get Willie Mays out the next day," Ford continued. "Originally, I didn't want to take the bet, but then I figured, what the hell. Willie came up and ripped the first two pitches I threw him deep but foul. I had him 0-2 and I figured that since it was an All-Star game and not a real game, I'd throw him a spitter. The ball started way inside and Willie headed for the dirt, just as the ball dropped in over the plate for a called third strike. Mickey went nuts in the outfield, cheering and applauding. Willie got kind of upset, because he thought Mick was showboating."

FOREIGN AFFAIRS

S am Snead played golf all over the world, although he always insisted that "anytime you leave America it's like camping out." He enjoyed visiting Africa, however, since it gave him a chance to do some big-game hunting, which he thoroughly enjoyed. On one such safari, he got into one of his more unusual matches.

"When I'd go off on one of these hunting trips, I'd always take along a couple of clubs and a few balls, just to keep my feel for the swing," Snead recalled. "Toward the end of one hunting trip, we had run out of golf balls so we had a little match using animal droppings that were about the size of golf balls. I had an edge, because when we were kids back home in Hot Springs we'd sell whatever balls we could find over at The Homestead and play with horse droppings. I figured out pretty quickly that the trick was hitting the dried-out side. The other guys never did figure that out, and I did pretty well for myself."

...

An American tourist visiting the British Isles showed up at Walton Heath and inquired with the club secretary if he might get a game. The secretary said he'd see what he could arrange and invited the tourist to have lunch.

Following lunch, the tourist was escorted to the first tee, where he was introduced to an older gentleman. They went out, had an enjoyable match for a few pounds, and repaired to the clubhouse for a post-round whiskey. After the elderly man left, the American sought out the club secretary to thank him for a lovely day.

"What a wonderful man," the American said of his playing partner. "He must have been a heck of a player in his prime."

"Indeed, he was, sir," the secretary said. "Mr. [James] Braid won the Open Championship five times."

...

If there is anything the Scots loathe, it's slow play—a particularly American tendency that drives the Scots to distraction.

On one occasion, an American visitor was playing in Scotland and from virtually the first hole his caddie started encouraging him to play faster. But since there was a lot of money riding on the match, the American played even more slowly than usual. Finally, his caddie had seen enough.

Facing a blind approach shot to a green, he asked his caddie for the line.

"See that ship's mast off in the distance," the caddie said. "That's your line."

The man hit a good-looking shot, but when they came down over the crest of the hill, the man saw that his ball was far wide of the green.

"I thought you said I should aim at the mast," the American said. "My shot covered it all the way."

"Aye," the caddie said, walking onward, "but it took you so long to play that the ship had sailed."

...

In the mid-1800s, a golfer from St. Andrews named

Allan Robertson was having dinner with a friend, Jamie Condie, another of Scotland's fine players. Condie was having a good-natured argument with Robertson, insisting that for all of Robertson's considerable skill, the secret to his success was his superior equipment. Naturally, Robertson disagreed, and they settled on a unique match for the following day.

The rules were simple: Each player would use the other's clubs. When a player won a hole, he would get to select and keep one of his opponent's clubs.

By the time they reached the home hole, Robertson had lost all of his clubs, save his two favorites—his driver and putter. When they walked off the last green, he had managed to lose his driver as well.

Desperate to get at least his driver back, he convinced Condie to play an extra hole.

Bad idea.

The extra hole cost him his putter as well.

...

The British love betting on sports and they particularly favor betting on golf.

In the run-up to the 1974 Masters, Trevor Homer,

the 1972 British Amateur champion, noticed that the bookmakers had set the odds of his winning the Masters at 5,000-1.

"Five million to one would be more bloody like it," he remarked.

But Homer noticed that bookies were offering odds of 3-1 that he wouldn't break 80 in his first two rounds. This was not an unreasonable bet, since in the previous year's Masters he shot rounds of 81-88 to miss the cut by a mile.

Homer placed a few pounds on himself, and then went out and shot rounds of 77-72. He missed the cut but came away a richer man for the experience—and for the bet.

...

An American writer was in Melbourne, Australia, for the 1988 World Cup of Golf. He soon struck up a friendship with a group of locals. One day they invited him to join them for a round of golf.

"What time?" the American asked.

"No worries," one of the Australians said. "We don't play until after four or five."

"Isn't that kind of a late start?" the American said.

"I meant beers, mate," the Australian said.

...

At the Sunningdale Golf Club outside London, the members have taken the notion of fair play to a remarkable level. According to the system known as the "Sunningdale handicap," when a player falls 2-down in a match, his opponent is required to give a stroke a hole until the match is squared.

BOB GOALBY

B ob Goalby won eleven times on the PGA Tour, but his greatest victory was the 1968 Masters. Sadly, that was the year Roberto De Vicenzo signed an incorrect scorecard and missed facing Goalby in a playoff for the green jacket. To this day there are people who mistakenly believe that Goalby's victory is somehow tarnished by De Vicenzo's disqualification. But in truth, no other action could have been taken—as De Vicenzo has always said whenever he is asked about the subject.

This was a huge story at the time, and it almost led to what would have certainly been a celebrated head-to-head match.

"One guy offered Bob and Roberto a $100,000 winner-take-all match," recalled Sam Snead years later. "Bob asked me what I thought, and I told him he should do it. People forget he was one of the best players on tour at the time. It would have been a helluva match, I'll tell you that. Well, it never happened because Cliff Roberts [the chairman of the Augusta National Golf Club] heard about it and put a stop to it."

JASON GORE

One of the happy sidebars to the 2005 U.S. Open at Pinehurst #2 was the emergence of Jason Gore, the player ranked 818th in the world who found himself tied for second place and in the final pairing going into the last round. Gore, thirty-one, is an over-size, happy-go-lucky guy who had a love affair with the huge galleries.

Gore was paired with two-time U.S. Open champion Retief Goosen, and while few people really expected Gore to win, what played out that Sunday afternoon was almost beyond belief.

Goosen, as steady a player as there is in the game, soared to an 11-over-par 81 while Gore shot an 84 to finish in a tie for forty-ninth.

As they stood on the sixteenth tee, the wreckage of

their rounds smoldering around them, Gore turned to Goosen and asked if he "wanted to play in for $10, just to make this interesting?"

Goosen laughed and took the bet. He won it when Gore double-bogeyed the final hole.

WALTER HAGEN

Walter Hagen was a genius when it came to match play, in part because he was a keen judge of people and a master of gamesmanship. No one knew this better than his longtime friend and rival Gene Sarazen.

The two went into the final round of a tournament tied for the lead and were paired together.

Prior to the round, a package was delivered to Sarazen's hotel room. It contained a bright orange tie and a note that read:

Dear Gene—
I'm sure you won't remember me but I'm the blonde from the Follies. Please wear this tie for good luck. I'll be in the gallery but don't look for me.

Sarazen played a poor front nine, his concentration divided between his golf and his search for the mysterious blonde. By the time they made the turn, heavy rain was falling, Hagen had a comfortable lead, and Sarazen had on a bright orange tie that was running down the front of his shirt.

Finally, Hagen could no longer contain himself.

"Kid, where'd you get that beautiful tie?" Hagen asked.

"From a friend," said Sarazen.

"Just a friend?" asked Hagen, who broke out laughing.

...

One time Hagen was playing a winner-take-all exhibition match when, late in the round, he hit his approach shot into a green-side bunker. When he reached the green, he saw that his ball had actually come to rest atop a paper bag that had blown into the hazard. He asked for a ruling and was told, inexplicably, that he was not allowed relief and had to either play the ball or declare it an unplayable lie and take a drop.

Hagen had other ideas.

He lit a cigarette, took a few deep drags, and then

placed the cigarette on the bag, which, moments later, burst into flames.

Hagen went on to hit a beautiful bunker shot and made his putt for par.

...

Hagen used to play a lot of lucrative exhibition tours with Joe Kirkwood, the great trick-shot artist from Australia. One such tour brought them to New York City.

After several postround drinks, they returned to their hotel, which was adjacent to Central Park. After another drink or two, Hagen challenged Kirkwood to a contest. They would open a window and hit balls into the park, then play back through the hotel. The player who pitched into the toilet bowl in the fewest strokes won the bet.

"We were pretty even until we reached the bathroom," said Kirkwood. "For some reason, Walter had a hell of a time getting the ball into the can."

...

Hagen was peerless when it came to gamesmanship—as Sam Snead discovered early in his career.

"We were having a little match and we came to this long par-three," Sam recalled. "I had the honor but I couldn't decide what club to hit. As I was trying to decide, out of the corner of my eye I saw Walter pull a fairway wood from his bag, so I took out my two-iron and airmailed the green. Walter just kind of smiled, gave me a wink, and put the wood back in the bag. It served me right."

E. J. "DUTCH" HARRISON

Dutch Harrison was a good player but, more importantly, he was one of the greatest scam artists the game has ever seen.

One of his favorite hustles was to show up in town and set up a series of matches with some of the local swells. Once he was well into their wallets, he'd offer to take his caddie—usually an uncommonly seedy-looking kid—as his partner and give them a chance to win back everything they had already lost. He'd even give them a few more strokes if necessary.

Another twist on this scam was for Harrison to seed the caddie yard with one of his caddies a couple of days ahead of his arrival. Then he'd set the hook.

"Boys, I want to give you a chance to get your money

back but I'm going to need a little help," he'd say. "Let me take that boy over yonder as my partner."

Then he'd motion the caddie over to the tee.

"Do you play golf, son?" he'd ask.

"Just a little," the caddie would reply.

"Well, go on over to my car and get my spare clubs and we'll give these fellows a match," Harrison would say.

With that, his caddie—Herman Keiser, who would go on to win the 1946 Masters—went out and did the best he could, which somehow was always good enough.

CLAYTON HEAFNER

Sam Snead once described Clayton Heafner as the "most even-tempered golfer I ever met. He's mad all the time."

Indeed, stories of Heafner's temper are the stuff of legend, like this one about his performance in a North Carolina tournament.

Heafner opened with a 66 but in the second round, with a large gallery following him, he hit a poor shot into the fifteenth hole. It was one bad shot too many, and he threw down his club and announced that he was picking up.

"Oh, no, Mr. Heafner, you can't do that," a woman said. "My husband and I bought you in the calcutta."

"OK, fine," said Heafner. "I won't pick up."

With that, he turned to his caddie.

"Go pick it up, boy," he said, and stormed back to the clubhouse.

BEN HOGAN

P aul Runyan won two PGA Championships, was
widely considered to be a short-game genius, and
was a highly respected teacher. He was already one of
the PGA Tour's stars when Ben Hogan came out on
tour, and they struck up a sort of mutual admiration
society based, in no small part, on their shared dedica-
tion to hard work and fascination with the intricacies of
the game.

Growing up in Hot Springs, Arkansas—which in
those days was something of a mecca for gamblers—
Runyan learned to play for money: sometimes a lot and
sometimes a little. Like Sam Snead, whom he trounced,
8 and 7, in the thirty-six-hole final of the 1938 PGA
Championship, he never needed to have a lot on the line
. . . just enough to keep things interesting.

Runyan often played matches with Hogan during practice rounds, and keeping score could be, to say the least, a complicated affair.

"Ben had a game that he really enjoyed," recalled Runyan. "It had nothing to do with the score you shot, but rather with the number of points you had at the end of the match. It was a little complicated, but basically you got points for hitting fairways and greens and a point for being closest to the hole on your approach shots. You lost points for missing a fairway or green, but if you missed the green and got up and down, you got a point. You lost a point if you hit a shot into a bunker, but you could redeem yourself by getting up and down.

"I wouldn't say Ben was an extravagant gambler, but he wasn't afraid to put his own money on the line," Runyan continued. "This was, of course, after he had become successful. Before then he didn't have any money to speak of. He went broke and had to leave the tour several times. One day Ben, Jackie Burke Jr., Bob McCallister, and myself were going to have a match. Ben wanted to play for $5 a point but I told him that simply was too rich for my taste. I told him I'd play for $1 a point, which was fine with him. Ben played by far the best golf that day and would have easily won the most money if we went by the score. But because of the nature of Ben's game, Jackie Burke won most of the money. Ben won a little and I think I lost about $16. Poor Bob McCallister lost $49, and, of course, he was the one who could least afford it."

...

While Hogan will forever be associated with Colonial Country Club, after his retirement from competition he played most of his golf at Shady Oaks, another club in Fort Worth.

Hogan preferred practicing to playing as he grew older, but he would occasionally play in matches, often with more than a little money on the side.

One competition involved "gangsomes," in which ten or fifteen middle- to high-handicappers would play as a group. Since the stakes were generally pretty high, one of the club members would recompute everyone's handicap after each match. According to Hogan's friends, while he would never give strokes to anyone in one-on-one competition, he grudgingly gave strokes in the gangsomes.

One variation on the gangsomes that Hogan particularly enjoyed was a game called "swing." In this game, players would pair off into two-man teams and one team would play against all the other teams.

On one memorable occasion, Hogan was paired with a wealthy friend of his who carried an eighteen handicap but rarely played to it—always a dangerous combination. On this day, Hogan and his partner got killed and Hogan demanded that everyone play the following day, with the bets doubled.

Legend has it that Hogan sought out the greens superintendent and arranged for the holes to be cut in the most precarious locations the following day. Hogan and his partner went out in the first group and Hogan shot a 62.

When the other teams came into the grillroom after their rounds, Hogan's customary snap-brimmed linen cap was sitting in the center of his favorite table, turned upside down so it could hold all the cash he and his partner had won—rumored to be some $20,000.

...

When Lanny Wadkins came out on the PGA Tour in the early 1970s, Ben Hogan was still playing in the occasional tournament. He took a liking to Wadkins and the two would play practice rounds together, with a little something riding on the outcome.

On one occasion, Wadkins beat Hogan, who paid off his bet with a check.

A few months later, Wadkins received a telephone call from Hogan's assistant.

"Mr. Wadkins," she said. "We've been reconciling Mr. Hogan's checking account and we notice that a check made out to you hasn't been cashed."

"Yes, ma'am," said Wadkins. "You tell Mr. Hogan that it's framed and posted on a wall in my office and will never be cashed."

...

Hogan was very fond of Tommy Bolt, and they often played casual rounds together (to the extent that Hogan ever played a truly *casual* round, or "happy golf," as he called it). One year at the Colonial National Invitational they were playing a practice round and came to the difficult, 176-yard, par-3 sixteenth. They disagreed about what club should be hit.

"I said it was a five-iron and Ben said it was a four,"

Bolt recalled. "We put a little bet down and I hit first, sneaking that little dude in there about twenty feet from the hole. Ben hit his four-iron inside me.

" 'See, Tommy, it was four,' Ben said.

" 'But you hit it fat,' I said.

" 'The shot called for a fat four,' Ben said."

...

Hogan and Toney Penna once teamed for a "casual" match against two friends.

On the first tee, Hogan told Penna that he could be captain of their team and decide which putts should be given. All went well for about four holes, at which point Penna conceded a short putt to Willie Goggin.

"That's it," Hogan said as they left the green. "You're not the captain anymore. We can't be giving away putts like that."

...

"I played a lot of matches with Ben," recalled Gardner Dickinson, who was Hogan's protégé. "He'd get on the first tee and put three balls down by the marker. If he wasn't satisfied with his first drive, he'd hit another. If he was happy with it, he'd say, 'That's it, boys. No mulligans today.' "

HUSBANDS AND WIVES

Three-time British Open champion Henry Cotton was playing in a friendly alternate-shot match. His partner was his wife, Toots.

On the first tee, Toots warned Henry that whatever else he did that day, he should take pains to see that he never left her a shot from the rough. Alas, on the second hole he pushed his drive into the right rough. Toots was furious and stormed down to the ball and whacked it back toward the tee. Nonplussed, Cotton simply addressed the ball with his 2-wood and hit a mighty blow that left the ball inches from the hole.

Toots was satisfied.

"Sometimes you just have to get Henry's attention," she quipped.

BOBBY JONES

Today, more than seventy-five years since he played his last competitive round, it is difficult to fathom just how dominant Bobby Jones really was in his time. Paul Runyan, a friend and contemporary of Jones, went to great lengths to give him his proper due.

"Walter Hagen would get angry with the other pros because he felt that they were intimidated by Bob," recalled Runyan. "And to a degree that was quite true. But he really was just that much better than everyone else. When he and I would play a friendly match, Bob would give me a stroke a side and I will be very candid with you and admit that I probably needed more than that. I had to play extremely well to beat Bob, even with the strokes.

"Tommy Armour had a similar arrangement with

Bob," Runyan added. "Bob would spot him a hole at the beginning of each nine. In other words, Tommy would begin each side one-up. When a writer asked Armour, who had tremendous pride, why he would agree to such an arrangement, he said it was because Bob was simply that good."

...

There were several reasons for Jones's decision to retire from competitive golf in 1930, at the age of twenty-eight. One reason, of course, was that he had won the Grand Slam—the U.S. and British Opens and Amateurs—and felt that, having done so, anything else would be anticlimactic. Another was that the pressures of golf at the highest level took a physical toll on him. There was also the issue of money: Jones, while comfortable, was not a wealthy man and felt the need to get on with his legal career.

A fourth and lesser-known reason was that Jones discovered how heavily many of his friends were betting on him during the championships. One friend, Henry Lapham, reportedly paid $23,000 to buy Jones in a calcutta at the 1929 U.S. Amateur at Pebble Beach. He also bought 1913 U.S. Open champion Francis Ouimet—who went on to win two U.S. Amateurs—for $8,000. Many people believe that this knowledge led to Jones's upset loss to Johnny Goodman—who traveled to California on a freight train—in an early round of the match play. Goodman was a relative unknown but went on to win the 1937 U.S. Amateur, as well as the 1933 U.S. Open, when he became the last amateur to win that national championship.

...

In 1928, Bob Jones and Walter Hagen met for a seventy-two-hole match designed to help promote a new golf course and raise money for local charities. Jones, who was younger than Hagen and at the top of his game, went off as a 3-2 favorite.

Hagen was 3-up after the morning eighteen, but it looked as though Jones might get one back when Hagen drove into the trees on the sixth hole in the afternoon round. With Jones in the center of the fairway, Hagen carefully studied his options and decided to try to slice the ball back into play. Instead, he topped the ball, barely getting it airborne. Of course,

Hagen being Hagen, the ball scooted under the branches, ran along the fairway and through a bunker, and came to rest ten feet from the hole. Jones made his par and then looked on in wonder as Hagen sank his birdie putt.

"I watched his shot from behind the trees and thought, 'Bob, you're four-down to a man who can miss a shot like that.' When a man misses a drive that badly, skulls his second shot, and then wins the hole with a birdie, it really gets your goat."

At the end of the first thirty-six holes, Hagen was 8-up on Jones. A week later, play resumed and Hagen went 9-up by sinking a sixty-foot birdie putt on the second hole. Hagen went on to shoot a 69 to Jones's 72, and by the end of that morning's play, Hagen was 12-up.

Playing the seventh hole in the afternoon, Hagen was 12-up with twelve holes to play. Jones chipped in, but it was only a momentary respite. Hagen chipped in on top of him.

Hagen collected $6,800 for his victory and promptly gave $5,000 to a St. Petersburg, Florida, hospital. He also presented Jones with a handsome set of cuff links.

Later, Jones summed up his feelings about Hagen.

"Many of the fellows find it difficult to play with Walter, but I enjoy it. He goes along with his chin up, smiling at everyone, and never complains about a bad break. He just plays the ball as he finds it, and goodness knows, he comes closer to beating luck itself than anyone I know."

...

After graduating from Georgia Tech at seventeen (he finished the four-year program in two and a half years), Jones studied English literature at Harvard. While he couldn't play golf for Harvard—he'd used up his collegiate eligibility at Georgia Tech—he gladly served as the team's manager. Happily, this role largely consisted of keeping an eye on the team's whiskey supply. Beyond that, he often practiced with the team and played exhibitions to raise funds for the team and for Harvard.

One day, during a practice session at The Country Club, he played against the six-man team's best ball—and won.

JOHN F. KENNEDY

President John F. Kennedy was a very good golfer, maybe the best golfer who ever held the office. When he vacationed in Florida, he would often play at the Seminole Golf Club with his longtime friend Chris Dunphy.

One day when they were playing, Kennedy hit a perfect drive and then knocked his 4-iron approach shot to within three feet of the hole. When they reached the green, he looked at Dunphy, waiting for him to concede the putt. He waited and waited and finally said, "C'mon Chris, certainly you're not going to make me putt this."

"Well, Mr. President, it's early in the round," Dunphy said. "Let's see what your stroke looks like today."

"OK, fine," Kennedy said, "but let's get going. I've got

a meeting with the head of the Internal Revenue Service right after we finish."

"It's good," said Dunphy, knocking the ball away.

...

The caddies at Seminole Golf Club have been known to bet on the outcome of the matches between their players, and on at least one occasion this involved President Kennedy.

It came to the closing holes of the match and Kennedy was reading his putt. Since it was customary for people to concede putts to the president, he wasn't exactly hurrying. Finally, his opponent had seen enough.

"That's good, Mr. President," the man said. "Pick it up."

"No!" said his caddie.

Kennedy looked over at him and broke out laughing.

PETER KESSLER

Peter Kessler is a reformed Wall Street guy who went on to enjoy a nice run as the host of The Golf Channel's *Golf Talk Live* interview show. Kessler was a single-digit handicapper who clearly relished the time he spent with players, both during the interviews and in occasional rounds of golf.

"Right after Ernie Els won the 1997 U.S. Open at Congressional, I played with him, fellow South African Fulton Allem, and Robert Baker, who was Ernie's teacher," recalled Kessler. "It was Fulton and me against them, and it proved to be no contest. Ernie made nine birdies and an eagle and Baker made six birdies. We wound up losing so much money that even today, I'm not really sure how much we lost."

LAWSON LITTLE

N ot many people today remember what a wonderful player Lawson Little was. He won the
1934 and 1935 U.S. Amateurs and then turned pro and
was one of the top players on tour during the 1940s. The
highlight of his professional career came in 1940, when
he won the U.S. Open by beating Gene Sarazen in a
playoff at Canterbury Golf Club.

If his win in the U.S. Open was the apex of his career,
his travails one year in the Seminole Pro-Am were easily
among his low points.

There was a huge calcutta at Seminole, and the
winner of the tournament would get about 10 percent of
the pot. Little and his partner came to the eighteenth
hole needing just a par to win. Since his amateur partner
was getting a stroke on the hole, it looked like a lock.

While Little played his way out of the hole (doubtless because he was thinking about his winnings), his partner hit his approach ten feet from the hole. Then he lagged his first putt a couple of inches from the hole.

Then disaster struck.

Thinking his putt was good, the amateur knocked it away—clear off the green. He wound up making a double-bogey, and Little wound up barely winning enough to cover his expenses.

JOE LOUIS

After his boxing career, which dominated the 1930s and 1940s, Joe Louis turned to golf and tried to make a living as a professional. While his fame got him a few invitations to play in PGA Tour events, most of his competition was on the old Negro Tour, where there were any number of very talented players. One of the best was Ted Rhodes, who liked and admired Louis but also knew a pigeon when he saw one.

One day they came to the final hole of a match and Louis asked his caddie how far he was from the hole.

"Champ," the caddie said. "You're about a bogey away and a $10 bill to Mr. Ted."

...

"Joe Louis was a good golfer," recalled Paul Runyan, "but to be quite honest, he was not nearly as good as he thought or other people claimed. A lot of people took advantage of Joe. One of them was Smiley Quick. He was a keen judge of human nature and he was very skilled at hustling Joe. People tried to warn Joe about Smiley, but Joe could be stubborn. Plus, as I said, he always had people around him telling him he was better than he really was. I have heard that Smiley bought two condominium complexes with just the cash he won from Joe, and I believe that to be absolutely true."

GEORGE LOW

George Low's father, George Sr., was a longtime professional at Baltusrol Golf Club in New Jersey, and George Jr. grew up to be a skilled, if not necessarily disciplined, player. He was, however, a brilliant putter who gained modest fame in the 1960s when Arnold Palmer credited him with turning his putting round.

Low once famously quipped, "Give me a millionaire with a fast backswing and I can have a very enjoyable afternoon."

Enter Edward, Duke of Windsor.

The duke is best known for giving up one of the all-time great jobs in the world—being the king of England—for one Mrs. Wallis Simpson, who had been around the track more often than Seabiscuit. He loved golf, but, like most other things in his life, he wasn't very good at it.

One day the duke found himself in the unlikely position of playing a match against George Low at Seminole. Their host was one of the duke's friends, Mr. Robert R. Young, a railroad tycoon.

Not surprisingly, Low dusted the duke and the tycoon. As they walked toward the clubhouse, Low kept waiting for the duke to cover his bets. When it became increasingly clear that the duke had no intention of paying up, the tycoon discreetly took Low aside.

"Perhaps I should have mentioned this earlier," said Mr. Young, "but the duke never pays off his wagers."

"He don't what?" asked an incredulous Low, who was beginning to feel the way the British people felt when the duke took a jump.

"His Royal Highness believes it's rather an honor to enjoy his company and, therefore, he shouldn't be required to pay something as banal as a bet," Mr. Young added.

"Mr. Young," said Low. "From now on, you take care of your railroads and I'll take care of my dukes."

DAVE MARR

Dave Marr came from a golf background. He grew up in Houston, where his father was a professional; so was his uncle, Jack Burke Sr. His cousin, Jackie Burke, was an outstanding player and a winner of both the Masters and the PGA Championship. Dave went on to win the 1965 PGA Championship and enjoyed a long and successful career as a television golf analyst.

"I really learned to play on the public courses in Houston," Marr often recalled. "You'd play money matches against guys who could really play. One of the best was Tommy Bolt. Man, people today forget just how good he was.

"In those days, nobody had much money, but you'd win all kinds of stuff in tournaments," Marr said.

"Guys would have their car trunks filled with toasters, televisions—everything imaginable. If you couldn't come up with the cash, you'd settle your bet with something from your trunk.

"This one day, I managed to nick Tommy pretty good and he was hot," Marr laughed. "Man, he stormed off the course and headed for the parking lot. I'm kind of hanging around the pro shop waiting for him to come back. A few minutes later he walks in with a shotgun he'd won the week before. You should have seen the assistant pros hit the floor when they saw Tommy come through the door."

CHARLES BLAIR MACDONALD

Charles Blair (C. B.) Macdonald was a good golfer, a superb course architect, and a wealthy and imperious man.

Macdonald founded the National Golf Links on New York's Long Island and ruled the place with an iron fist. Autocratic to a fault, he had a wonderful approach to members who made suggestions. If he disliked the idea, he simply ignored it. If he thought the suggestion had merit, he simply ordered the work done and then billed the member.

Macdonald's nephew was Peter Grace, who, by all indications, was like his uncle in almost every way.

One day Grace came off the course after playing it for the first time. His uncle asked Grace what he thought, and Grace—keeping in character—said he thought it was too easy. His criticism began with the first hole, which he said was too short and could easily be driven.

"Don't be ridiculous, Peter," Macdonald said. "No one has even come close to driving that green. It's nonsense. I'll wager you any amount that you can't drive the green."

With that, they headed for the first tee, where Grace hit what might be the most expensive shot in golf history. The ball tore off the clubface, burned through the wind, landed short of the green, and ran onto the putting surface.

Macdonald was horrified—and livid. He stormed back to the clubhouse. Later that night, he wrote Grace out of his will—which meant that Grace's magnificent tee shot cost him about $1 million.

THE MASTERS

In the early years of the Masters Tournament, calcutta betting pools were an integral part of the week's festivities.

In 1948, when Claude Harmon's name came up, it didn't draw much action. After all, even though he was a good player, he was at a point of his career where he was better known for his teaching—which made sense, since he was one of the best teachers in the country.

In the end, a man bought Harmon for $450. When Harmon won, the man collected more than $10,000.

PHIL MICKELSON

Phil Mickelson, the 2004 Masters champion, is well known for his no-holds-barred approach to the game. It is often said he never saw a pin he wouldn't shoot at, and that's made him one of the most popular players on the PGA Tour.

Mickelson is also known as a player who seldom—if ever—backs off from a challenge, and that includes a bet. One of his most successful came in a practice round at the 1998 Masters.

It seems that John Daly and Tim Herron were going to join Mickelson and John Huston for a pair of practice rounds. Each player is known for his ability to run off impressive strings of birdies, but it was Mickelson and Huston who got on a roll and stayed there. By the

time the dust had settled, Mickelson and Huston had won $27,000.

"It was great," recalled Mickelson. "Without a doubt the best practice rounds I've ever played. In fact, they were the first practice rounds I was ever excited to play."

...

In the 2001 World Golf Championships–NEC Invitational, Tiger Woods and Jim Furyk went at each other in a long and dramatic playoff. At one point, Furyk faced a difficult bunker shot.

"Twenty-five-to-one says he holes it," said Mickelson to the players gathered around a television set in the locker room. "Who wants that for $20?"

It seemed like a pretty safe bet to Mike Weir . . . who wound up paying Mickelson $500 when Furyk holed the bunker shot.

DR. CARY MIDDLECOFF

D oc Middlecoff was one of the best players in the world during the 1940s and 1950s, winning thirty-nine PGA Tour events, including the Masters and the U.S. Open. Doc wasn't much of a gambler, but he did enjoy a challenge. Usually he managed to win money, although on one memorable occasion he came up on the short end of a money match.

"When I was about nineteen or twenty, I used to play at a place called LaGorce, up in Hollywood, Florida," recalled Doug Sanders. "There were more betting games up there than you could shake a stick at and Doc was a regular. He had the most unbelievable caddie in the world. This is before we played by yardage. You went by what your eye told you, and this guy was phenomenal. He'd tell Doc exactly what club to hit and how to hit it. He might say, 'Hit a five-iron and take off three yards,' or 'Hit the seven and add two yards.' He knew Doc's game inside and out and Doc trusted him completely. He was the best I ever saw. Well, one day I had a big match lined up with Doc so I went to this guy at LaGorce and paid him a few bucks to fix some pins. He'd cut about a foot and a half or two feet off of some of the pins and added it to the others. Then he replaced the regular pins with the ones he doctored. If a hole was cut on the front of the green, just over a bunker, he'd put the long pin in the cup. Doc and his caddie would look at the pin and figure it was about 135 yards and a nine-iron to the hole, when it was really 30 yards less. He was in the front bunkers all day. If the hole was cut toward the back of the green, he'd use the short pin and Doc's approach shots would still be rising when they went over the greens. It wasn't long before the caddie was completely confused and Doc was getting all over his back.

"Twenty years later, I ran into the caddie and he told me that was the worst day he ever had.

" 'Doug,' he said. 'I've never been that bad at judging distances in my whole life. I don't know what the hell happened. I gave Doc the wrong club every time.'

"You should have seen his expression when I told him what had happened," said Sanders.

BYRON NELSON

Ken Venturi, the 1964 U.S. Open champion and longtime golf analyst for CBS Sports, worked with Byron Nelson as an amateur and generously credits Nelson with much of his success. When asked who he believes is the greatest player he ever saw, he gives due respect to the likes of Bob Jones, Ben Hogan, Sam Snead, Jack Nicklaus, and the rest, but he saves his highest praise for Nelson.

"You can debate who was the greatest player in history and never come up with an answer," said Venturi. "But if you ask who was the greatest gentleman in the history of the game, there's only one choice: Byron Nelson."

Nelson is a gentleman, and he is also a gentle man. Still, he's as competitive as any player in history, especially when provoked.

For a time, Nelson was the golf professional at the Inverness Club in Toledo, Ohio. One of the members was Frank Stranahan, the heir to the Champion spark plug fortune and one of the top amateurs of his time; he won two British Amateurs, among other titles. That Stranahan had a high opinion of his own game is putting it mildly.

Stranahan frequently challenged Nelson to a match, but Nelson always declined, figuring, properly, that it was a no-win situation. Stranahan, however, wouldn't give up and finally pushed Nelson too far. Nelson accepted the match, adding that not only would he play Stranahan, but he'd also play the best ball of Stranahan and two of his low-handicap friends.

They never knew what hit them. Nelson shot a record 63 on a course that went on to host three U.S. Opens and a PGA Championship.

...

Byron Nelson was renowned for the accuracy of his shots. Jack Nicklaus often recalls watching an exhibition Nelson put on in advance of a U.S. Junior Amateur Championship.

"The course had a new watering system and you could see the line where the irrigation pipes had been laid down the center of the fairway," Nicklaus said. "Byron started hitting short irons and made his way through the bag. Every single ball hit on that line."

Just how accurate was he?

When Nelson first came east from Texas to start his professional career, he took a job as the assistant pro at Ridgewood Country Club in New Jersey. Word of his talent soon spread among the membership. One day a man approached Nelson in the pro shop.

"Byron, I'll bet you that you can't hit that flagpole down there," the man said, pointing.

Nelson grabbed a 1-iron, walked to the first tee, addressed the ball, and hit the flagpole with his first shot.

JACK NICKLAUS

J ack Nicklaus occupies a unique place in golf, both for his playing record and for his supreme sportsmanship. As his friend and longtime rival Gary Player has said, "As great as Jack is in victory, he is even better in defeat." It is a statement that no one who follows the game could even think of arguing with.

It goes without saying that Nicklaus is a magnificent competitor, but few stories illustrate this as well as this one told by Tom Weiskopf, whose relationship with Nicklaus goes back to their days at Ohio State.

"Jack and I would go over to the British Open a week early to play practice rounds together," said Weiskopf, who won the 1973 British Open. "At Carnoustie in 1975, we went out to play after dinner, which you could do because it stays light so late in the summer in Scotland.

We were on the second green when we heard [Australia's] Jack Newton and John O'Leary, an Irish professional, calling to us from the tee. We waited for them and when they reached the green, they challenged us to a match. Nicklaus wasn't really interested. In fact, he seldom had a bet on a practice round because he wasn't trying to shoot a score. He was just trying to fit his game to how the course was playing.

"There was a gallery of several hundred people around, and they could hear almost everything that was being said. Newton kept at us, saying that we were two of the best players in the world but we were afraid to play them. Jack just kind of ignored them and went about his business. Newton birdied three and then ran in a forty-footer for birdie on number four. Jack Newton is a great guy, but he got pretty full of himself and asked if we wanted to press. Now you have to remember that we hadn't even agreed to a match.

"I'd known Jack for a long time, and he shot Newton a look I had never seen before or since. He put those blues on Newton and said, 'Jack, we aren't two-down yet.' With that, he ran in a ten-footer for birdie.

"All of a sudden, Nicklaus says we're playing for $10 automatic one-downs. No discussion or anything. We get to the fifth tee and he takes me aside and says, 'Tom, if you've ever really tried in your life, I want you to try now. I want to bury these guys.'

"I've seen Jack pretty intense, but never as intense as he was that night. Between the two of us we made twelve birdies and an eagle over the next fourteen holes. But the story gets even better. On the eighth hole, which is one of the hardest par-threes you'll ever see, Jack hit first. We knew it was a good shot, so I decided to shoot right at the flag. The ball covered the pin all the way and the gallery applauded politely, but because the pin was partially blocked by some mounds, we couldn't see where the ball wound up. When we reached the green, we saw three balls, but none of them was mine. Finally, Nicklaus went over and pulled my ball from the hole.

" 'Can you believe it? You made a hole-in-one and no one said anything.'

"With that he walked over to these two old Scots sitting on shooting sticks and asked them if they had seen the ball go in the hole.

" 'Aye, Jack,' one of the guys said. 'But isn't this just a practice round?' "

...

One of the things that comes with being Jack Nicklaus is that everyone wants to take a shot at you.

Back in the late 1960s, the old Thunderbird Classic—now the Barclays Classic—was played at Westchester Country Club in the New York City suburb of Harrison, New York. At the time, there was a local player named Jack DiPaolo whose length off the tee was legendary. In fact, at one point *Golf Digest* put him on its cover.

On one occasion, Mr. DiPaolo (and perhaps some of his friends) thought it would be a good idea to challenge Nicklaus to a test of power on the club's polo field, which served as the practice range for the tournament.

The challenge was simple: ten shots at $1,000 each. Longest shot wins.

According to local caddie legend, Nicklaus considered the bet and made a counteroffer: one swing for $10,000.

Mr. Jack DiPaolo wisely declined.

...

"My kids and I always made lists of the three living people we would each like to meet," explained the late Dick Fisher, the former chairman and CEO of Morgan Stanley. "It wasn't enough just to say hello to them and shake their hands. You had to actually get to know the people. Jack was on my list, along with John Updike and Willem de Kooning.

"Phil Purcell, the CEO of Morgan Stanley, knew how much I wanted to meet Jack, so he arranged a game for the three of us, plus Ed Telling from Sears, at Seminole, which is near Jack's home in Florida. Seminole is one of my favorite courses because, depending on the wind, it plays differently every day.

"I was very nervous, but Jack put us immediately at ease. We discussed my polio and I was surprised to learn that both Jack and his sister, Marilyn, had contracted polio as kids. It had no lingering effects on Jack, although Marilyn's case was a bit more severe.

"Jack impressed me right from the beginning. We were warming up on the practice range and Jack was hitting five-woods into the screen at the far end of the range. Some people were urging Jack to pull out his driver.

" 'Could you hit it over the screen?' one man asked Jack.

" 'Of course I could,' Jack said. 'But you're not supposed to.'

"That impressed me, and what happened on the first tee impressed me even more," Fisher continued. "Phil suggested that Jack play from the championship tees, but Jack declined.

" 'We're just going to have a friendly game,' Jack said. 'Let's play from the same markers.'

Next, someone suggested a $100 nassau, which we could all afford. Jack begged off.

" 'Let's keep it fun,' Jack said, suggesting a $2 nassau.

"Obviously, Jack could have easily handled a $100 nassau and the odds are pretty good he would have made some money, but that wasn't what he was all about," Fisher continued. "I'm a pretty competitive person and I like to play with something on the line, but I've never understood people who gamble for large sums of money on the course. I think they're missing the point of the game. One day I was playing at Winged Foot and there was a group behind us that seemed to be yelling and cheering on every hole. Finally, when they putted out on the eighteenth, there was an enormous amount of shouting. My curiosity got the better of me and when they came into the clubhouse, I asked them what all the yelling was about. It turned out that one man had just made a twelve-footer that was worth $16,000. That's a little rich for my blood.

"Anyway, we had a wonderful match and, of course, it was a great thrill to watch Jack up close. I got a glimpse of what makes him so great on the 175-yard, par-three seventeenth, a classic hole that runs along the Atlantic.

" 'It's either a six or a seven,' Jack said to his caddie, before pulling the seven-iron out of his bag.

" 'Hit the six,' the caddie said.

" 'There's one difference between you and me,' Jack said to the caddie. 'I'm the one who has to hit the shot.'

"And he hit it about five feet from the hole," said Fisher.

...

Nicklaus earned an invitation to the 1960 Masters by virtue of his victory in the 1959 U.S. Amateur.

He was already a hero in his hometown of Columbus, Ohio, and a number of his friends made the trip to Augusta to watch him play. Just to make the week interesting, they came up with a bet.

They would take Nicklaus against any other twenty players. If Nicklaus beat those twenty players, Jack's friends won money from those they bet with. If any player on someone's twenty-player team beat Jack, that person would win.

Nicklaus wound up finishing tied for thirteenth and was the low amateur. He *and* his friends had a very enjoyable week.

...

Spyglass Hill, a treacherous Robert Trent Jones design, was added to the rota for the old Bing Crosby National Pro-Am in 1967. Having played the course, Crosby made a bet with Jack Nicklaus.

"Jack," Crosby said. "I've got five that says you can't shoot par from the back tees the first time you play the course." Nicklaus accepted the challenge and shot a smooth 2-under-par 70.

"By the way, Bing, was that five dollars or five thousand?" Nicklaus asked Crosby when he saw him later.

They settled on $500.

...

Prior to the start of the 1960 U.S. Open, Charlie Nicklaus approached his son and mentioned that the odds of his winning the championship were set at 35-1. He asked Jack if they should place a bet.

"Darned right," said Jack. "Put down $20."

"Win, place, or show?" Charlie asked.

"Win," said Jack.

He came close, finishing second to Arnold Palmer.

...

By all accounts, Jack Nicklaus is a wonderful father . . . but that doesn't mean he cuts his kids any slack on the golf course.

"Jack loves playing with the kids," said his wife, Barbara. "But I can't tell you how many times he'd come to the last hole in a match with them and have a putt to win. He'd look at whoever it was and say, 'I hate to do this to you, but . . .' and then he'd sink his putt. I mean, he even does it to me when we play."

MOE NORMAN

Many people believe that the late Moe Norman was the purest ball striker who ever lived. Be that as it may, he was also one of the most eccentric players in the history of the game.

One year Norman was leading a tournament coming to the final hole. He asked his caddie how long the hole was.

"For you, it's a driver and a nine-iron," said the caddie.

Norman walked to the tee and hit his 9-iron into the fairway. When he reached his ball, he took his driver and knocked it onto the green, then made his putt for a birdie.

On another occasion, Norman came to the final hole, again leading the tournament. When he reached the tee, he asked an official what first prize was.

"A beautiful toaster oven," the man said.

"What's second prize?" Moe asked.

"A radio," the official said.

With that, Norman went on to double-bogey the hole and finish second.

"What was I going to do with another toaster oven?" Norman said later. "I've already got twenty-seven of them."

...

One time Norman was playing in a tournament. The course was backed up and Norman was idly bouncing a ball off the face of his driver.

"I'll pay you $1 for every bounce over 100," a spectator said.

With the gallery counting, Norman bounced the ball off his driver 184 times before he took pity on the man, who had grown ashen-faced.

"I could have gone all afternoon, but I didn't want to hold up the tournament," Norman said.

THOMAS P. "TIP" O'NEILL

Tip O'Neill, the former Speaker of the House of Representatives, loved the game of golf. He learned it as a boy, caddying at the clubs around his native Cambridge, Massachusetts. In fact, one day he caddied for no less a figure than Bobby Jones.

Tip may not have been the best golfer that ever lived, but he loved to tell stories about the game, and one of his favorites concerned a round he played with Sam Snead.

"One day I'm playing golf with Sammy Snead and a couple of guys named Kelly down at Pine Tree in Florida," said O'Neill. "We get on the first tee and they tell me we're going to play a $20 nassau, which is a little rich for my tastes but I figure, what the hell, I'm playing with the great Sammy Snead.

"Well, to be perfectly honest with you, I got beat pretty good but it didn't bother me a bit because we had a great time. After lunch, we decided to play a little gin. Now, I'm a pretty good gin player. As a matter of fact, I'm one of the best, and I won back everything I lost plus a little extra. When we finished, Sammy stood up, shook my hand, and said "O'Brien, you're a helluva fella. What'd you say you do for a living?"

...

Tip O'Neill had a wonderful sense of humor and never took the game too seriously. Witness the time during the Bob Hope Classic when he found himself unable to get the ball out of deep bunker and, on national television, finally picked the ball up and tossed it onto the green.

One of his favorite stories concerned a round at the Hope when he was paired with Lee Trevino.

"We're going along and I'm playing pretty good," O'Neill said, "which was good because we had a little bet going with one of the other teams. We get to this par-three over water and I take out an old ball and toss it down on the tee.

" 'What are you doing?' Trevino asked me. 'Put down a new ball and let's see a good practice swing.'

"I figured this guy's one of the best players in the world, so he must know what he's talking about. I put down a new ball and made a couple of practice swings.

" 'Hold on,' Trevino said, bending down and picking up my ball. 'Hit the old one.' "

ARNOLD PALMER

No one has ever had more patience with golf fans—or had more dinners interrupted by people who wanted an autograph—than Arnold Palmer. But on at least one occasion even Palmer was pushed over the edge.

"Arnold genuinely likes people, which I think he got from his father, who was a club pro," said Dave Marr, one of Palmer's closest friends on tour. "You really had to work at it to get Arnold mad, but one night at P.J. Clarke's in New York, Arnold and Winnie were having dinner with Frank Gifford and his wife and some guy at the next table—who had probably had a little bit too much to drink—was trying to goad Arnold. He knew Arnold was leaving the next day to go overseas because it had been in the papers, so he kept challenging Arnold, saying that there wasn't that much difference between a tour pro and a good amateur, which he apparently was. Then he challenged him to a $500 nassau at any local course if Arnold would give him one stroke a side.

"Arnold was very patient about the whole thing and told the man that as much as he'd like to play him, he had to leave the next day. Well, the hero turns to his friends and starts bragging about how he'd just backed down the great Arnold Palmer. That did it. Arnold swiveled in his chair and looked the guy straight in the eye.

" 'I'll see you tomorrow morning at Winged Foot,' said Palmer. 'I'll give you two a side and we're going to play a $5,000 nassau. Are we on?'

"Frank said you could hear the guy gulp from across the room. He just looked down at the table and didn't say another word."

...

Even as a kid, Arnold Palmer enjoyed a challenge.

His father, Deacon, was the golf professional at the Latrobe Country Club in Pennsylvania, and Arnold loved to spend time on the course. Happily, he found a way to be out on the course *and* earn a little extra money.

On Ladies' Day, he would wait on the tee of a hole

that required a drive over a large pond. As a foursome would arrive on the tee, he'd offer the women a bet: he'd hit their drives for them and, if the ball carried the hazard, they'd pay him a quarter; if he failed, he'd supply them with a new ball.

...

Pine Valley Golf Club has a storied place in golf history as one of the finest courses in the world, but it also played an important role in Arnold Palmer's long and happy marriage to Winnie.

Palmer was just out of the Coast Guard and already had a reputation as an outstanding amateur golfer. He had heard a lot about Pine Valley but had never played the course. One day he was invited to play, but his friends warned him not to expect to score very well on his first attempt.

Now, at the time, Arnold very much wanted to marry Winnie, but he didn't have the money for a nice engagement ring. As luck would have it, his friends offered him a bet: for every stroke over 80, Palmer would have to pay them $100, but they'd pay him $100 for every stroke under 80.

Palmer turned in a smooth 68, pocketed $1,200, bought the ring, and lived happily ever after.

…

Hackers from coast to coast and probably around the world believed that even if they couldn't swing a club like Sam Snead, they could play the game with Arnold Palmer's reckless abandon. This bravura often met with disastrous results. Take the case of a first-time guest at Augusta National who showed up shortly after the Masters one year.

Much to his delight, he drew the same caddie who had looped for Palmer earlier that year. The group decided on a $100 nassau, and off they went. The first nine was halved, which meant there was at least $300 riding on the back nine, and the match remained tied through fourteen holes. On the par-5 fifteenth, the guest hit his best drive of the day.

"This is where Arnie was," the caddie told his player as they pondered their second shot.

That was probably not the best thing to tell his player just at that moment.

"What did he hit?" the man asked.

"He hit his four-iron," the caddie said.

"Give me the four."

Moments later, he hit a very good 4-iron . . . and watched in despair as the ball splashed into the pond fronting the green.

"Are you sure he hit a four-iron?" the man asked.

"Yes sir, he did," the caddie said. "And he hit it in the water, too."

...

"One of the things I loved about playing on tour were the matches we'd have during practice rounds," recalled Tom Weiskopf, the 1973 British Open champion. "One that really stands out is a match at Harbour Town, where Arnold and I played Lanny Wadkins and Bert Yancey.

"Our usual bet was $20 automatic one-downs, and that day we finished the first eighteen around two o'clock and Arnold and I had gotten clipped pretty good, so Arnold insists that we play another nine to see if we can get back to even. After the next nine, we're still down and Lanny is getting all over us. Arnold is adamant that we're going to go another nine. By this time, it's about four-thirty and I don't think we're going to have enough daylight to get in another nine. Arnold didn't care. He was going to play until we caught up, so off we went. We played the last few holes in the dark and Arnold and I still lost. He couldn't believe it."

...

Although Palmer has cut back on his PGA Tour and Champions Tour schedules, he still enjoys friendly matches at his Bay Hill Club & Lodge in Orlando, Florida. The Shootout, as it's known, was a fixture well before Palmer became involved with the ownership and operation of the club. Not surprisingly, given the number of tour pros who live in the Orlando area, the Shootout is popular with them as well as with the amateurs who play in it regularly.

On an average day, the participants gather for lunch and then divide into ten or so four-man teams, each of which includes an "A," "B," "C," and "D" player based upon handicaps. Each player pays a $30 entry fee (sometimes higher for special events) and the players on the winning team usually pocket a couple hundred dollars, which, according to tradition, is used to buy drinks for the field in the grillroom. In addition, there are all sorts of side bets, just to make things even more interesting. On New Year's Eve, the Shootout attracts a couple hundred players and a very handsome pot.

One day Palmer came to the difficult, par-3 seventeenth hole with a lot of bets on the line. With 210 yards over water to the hole, Palmer asked his longtime caddie, Tomcat, for his 2-iron.

"No sir, it's only a three today," said the caddie.

Palmer insisted he needed a 2-iron to get back to the hole but let himself get talked into a 3-iron. He hit it beautifully, but watched in dismay as it splashed into the lake short of the green.

Naturally, his playing companions broke up, which inspired Palmer to even greater determination.

"Tomcat, that was the wrong damn club," Palmer said. "Now give me the two-iron."

Armed with his 2-iron, Palmer told the group he was going to "make par the hard way."

That's exactly what he did, holing the 2-iron for his par.

"See, Tomcat," Palmer said, triumphantly. "I told you it was a two-iron."

"No it wasn't," the caddie said. "You hit that fat. It was still a three-iron."

PINE VALLEY

P ine Valley is without question one of the greatest courses in the world, but it can be hell on earth if you stray from the straight and narrow.

One time a player came down for a weekend with friends. It was his first visit to the club, and naturally some fairly hefty matches were arranged. When he shot a smooth 79 on Saturday, he and his partner cleaned up.

The next day, however, was a different story. With all the bets doubled, he found himself in some of the more exotic parts of the course. Days later, a friend asked him what happened.

"I found out where the trouble is," he answered.

GARY PLAYER

South Africa's Gary Player is one of just five players—the others are Gene Sarazen, Ben Hogan, Jack Nicklaus, and Tiger Woods—to win all four major professional championships.

It is safe to say that few—if any—players ever worked harder on their game than Player labored on his. And there has never been anyone who had more belief in himself or the power of positive thinking: witness his remarkable victory over Tony Lema in a semifinal of the World Match Play championship at the Wentworth Club in England.

After the morning eighteen of the thirty-six-hole match, Player found himself seven down and in very real danger of being humiliated. This was precisely the sort of challenge that fueled Player throughout his career, and he steeled himself for the make-or-break afternoon round.

By the end of the front nine, Player had cut Lema's lead to five up, then won the tenth hole with a par. By the time he won the eleventh with a birdie, the gallery, which had deserted the match in the morning, returned in droves—inspiring Player even more.

On the par-4 thirteenth hole, Player hit a magnificent drive while Lema hooked his tee shot into the woods and had no choice but to pitch back into play. Lema's third shot came up short of the hole, while Player hit a fine approach and had a ten-footer for birdie. Trying desperately to stanch the bleeding, Lema made a brave par putt and then stood aside to see if Player would make yet another birdie.

He did, and he was now just two down, with five holes to play.

They halved the next two holes and then, on the dangerous sixteenth, Player gambled and hit a driver from the tee. It was perfect, and moments later Lema—who was now visibly struggling—hit a 3-wood in a desperate attempt to find the fairway. Instead, he hit another hook into trouble, and Player cut the margin to just one.

On seventeen, Lema seemed to regain his poise and

made a key putt, putting the pressure back on Player, who needed to make a putt of his own for the halve and to keep his courageous comeback hopes alive. Player made the putt and remained one down.

On the par-5 eighteenth, Lema's second shot came up shy of the putting surface. Now it was Player's turn. Trying to hit the green in two, his shot sailed to the right and rattled into the trees. Player watched the shot with a grim expression on his face for what must have felt like an eternity before hearing a roar from the gallery and watching in amazement—and considerable relief—as the ball caromed out of the trees and rolled toward the hole. Lema, who by this time was totally unnerved, left his pitch well short of the hole and watched in dismay as Player made his putt to square the match.

The sudden-death playoff was a foregone conclusion. Player won on the first hole for what to this day he calls one of his greatest victories.

NICK PRICE

Zimbabwe's Nick Price is one of the most popular players on tour and, for a stretch in the 1990s, one of the best players in the world. Coming into the 2005 season, he had won eighteen tour events, including the 1994 British Open and two PGA Championships.

Two of the reasons for Price's popularity are his sense of humor and his easy good nature. Witness this story from his youth: Price was drafted into the Rhodesian Air Force, and as he reached the end of his physical exam, the doctor asked him if there were any medical reasons why he couldn't serve in the military.

"I do have this skin condition," he told the doctor.

"What's the problem?" the doctor asked.

"Bullets go through it," Price said.

...

"I was playing an exhibition match with Simon Hobday, Dale Hayes, and Mark McNulty in the early 1980s," Price recalled. "Mark and I were partners and at that time, he was one of the greatest putters in the world. He had an old Bullseye model that had been discontinued. I remember that it had a blue grip that was very distinctive. He was a magician with that putter and he guarded it very carefully, since it was virtually irreplaceable. Well, as luck would have it, Simon was poking around in the pro shop and he came across virtually the identical putter in a used-club barrel. It even had a blue grip. Simon bought it and snuck it into Mark's bag, putting Mark's putter aside.

"Now, you have to picture the scene," Price continued. "There were about two thousand people gathered around the first tee as we're being introduced by Dale. When it was time to introduce Mark, he said, 'Most of you know Mark for his incredible putting skill . . .' With that, Simon walked over to Mark's bag and said, 'Where is that bloody putter?' He pulled the putter out of Mark's bag and snapped it over his knee. The gallery gasped and Mark almost went into shock. I thought he was going to go after Simon on the spot. I'm still not sure he ever quite got over it."

CLIFFORD ROBERTS

C lifford Roberts was the longtime chairman of the Augusta National Golf Club and was an autocrat in the truest sense of the word. His word was pretty much law and what he said pretty much went.

One day his playing partner called in sick and Roberts asked one of the assistant pros to fill in for him. The young pro played pretty well, making nine straight pars. Imagine the pro's surprise when they made the turn and Roberts ordered him back to the pro shop.

"We don't need any more pars," Roberts said. "What we need is birdies. Why don't you go into the shop and see if you can't find someone who can make some birdies. When you do, send him out."

BOB ROSBURG

One evening over dinner, Dave Marr was talking about some of the players he had known in the course of his long playing and broadcasting career. When he came to Bob Rosburg, the winner of the 1959 PGA Championship and a longtime partner of Marr's at ABC Sports, he was effusive in his praise.

"Rossie was the most natural golfer I ever met," said Marr, who quickly added that Sam Snead didn't count because the Slammer was, in Marr's words, "supernatural."

Growing up in San Francisco, Rosburg made a name for himself as a twelve-year-old when he beat Ty Cobb in the finals of the club championship at the Olympic Club. This so infuriated the hypercompetitive Cobb that he promptly quit the club.

Like many players of his era, Rossie wasn't averse to

playing matches in which the stakes sometimes got a little high.

"After I turned pro, I used to come back to San Francisco for some pretty good matches," Rossie recalled. "There were these guys that were pretty well off and they'd arrange matches where $3,000 or $4,000 would change hands, which was pretty good money in those days but not so much that anyone could get hurt. We'd get about 25 percent of whatever our backers won, which was pretty good. Sometimes they'd bring Raymond Floyd in to play, too. He was just a kid but even then he loved the action. I think it made him a better player under pressure. Anyway, we played all the great courses around San Francisco and they were good matches. The amateurs were halfway decent but they were just out there to have fun. The funny thing is, sometimes after a match we'd go out and play with just two clubs each, and they were better with two clubs than they were with fourteen!"

PAUL RUNYAN

Two-time PGA champion Paul Runyan more than made up for his lack of size and distance with a keen mind, a burning competitive drive, and a brilliant short game. More than anything else, he knew his strengths and weaknesses.

"I was playing a match against a man who was a far longer hit than I was," Runyan recalled. "I hadn't been driving the ball particularly well and we came to the final hole of the match, which required a drive of some considerable length to carry a gorge from the championship tee. I wasn't sure I could carry it, but I noticed that the forward tee was fairly good-sized, so I pitched the ball down onto that tee, hit my brassie down the fairway, pitched up, and made my par. The long hitter was so shaken that he missed his putt and I was able to win."

...

Runyan was extremely competitive and always wanted to play for something.

"I don't care whether it's chalk, marbles, or money," he often said. "I just need to have something on the line to hold my attention."

He did, however, have one rule.

"I insist that if I lose, my opponent must accept my money," Runyan explained. "If they won't, I will never play with them again."

In the course of his long life, this only happened once.

"I was playing at Hillcrest Country Club in Los Angeles with Jimmy Durante and two of his friends," he recalled. "I wound up losing $25 to a man named Lou Clayton. I tried to pay him, but he said he wouldn't take my money because it had been a privilege to play with me. I told him that I appreciated that, but if he didn't accept my money I would never play with him again. I don't think he believed me, and he wouldn't accept my money. I never played with him again."

BABE RUTH

In 1941, Fred Corcoran—one of the greatest golf promoters and raconteurs in golf history—arranged for a fifty-four-hole match between Babe Ruth and Ty Cobb.

Initially, Cobb declined to play in the so-called "Ruth Cup." At fifty-four, he was six years older than Ruth and didn't have any interest in being involved in what would almost certainly be a media circus, given the involvement of both Ruth and Corcoran.

Not to be deterred, Corcoran sent a telegram to Cobb under Ruth's name. It read:

If you want to come out here and have your brains knocked out, come on.

—Babe

For good measure, Corcoran leaked the telegram to some friendly sportswriters.

The first eighteen holes were played at Commonwealth Country Club near Boston. Cobb won, 3 and 2, and then launched a jab at his old rival.

"The fat man is getting fatter," said Cobb. "He looks out of balance, like an egg resting on two toothpicks."

Ruth rallied in the second match, winning at Fresh Meadow Country Club in Flushing, New York. This set up a glorious final scheduled for Grosse Isle Country Club in Detroit.

As a solid six handicap, Cobb was a better player than Ruth, who possessed power to spare but was lacking in the finesse department. Still, Cobb wasn't taking any chances.

He hired Walter Hagen as his coach.

He hired the club's assistant pro as his caddie.

He tipped the staff to make sure that Ruth had plenty to drink during the boat ride to Detroit.

Not surprisingly, Ruth arrived on the first tee nursing a hangover of, well, Ruthian proportions.

By the time they made the turn, Ruth was still hung over and was also 5-down. Cobb offered to let Ruth press.

"How much?" Ruth asked.

"How about $50,000?" said Cobb.

Ruth wisely settled for less, which was just as well because Cobb won 3 and 2.

…

Babe Ruth was vacationing in Bermuda when he was invited to play the Mid Ocean Club, the sublime C. B. Macdonald design. Naturally he jumped at the chance.

Everything was going along swimmingly until he came to the 370-yard, par-4 fifth hole, which requires a drive over water. Since it is a fairly short hole, there really isn't much point in gambling, especially so early in a match.

Not that it mattered to Ruth, who looked at every tee shot as a chance to blow one out of the park. Against the advice of his caddie, he pulled his driver from the bag.

"I could throw it onto the green from here," he said.

Not quite. Fifteen balls went into the water before Ruth successfully reached the fairway. That was enough for him. Ruth walked in and repaired to the clubhouse bar for an afternoon of solace.

DOUG SANDERS

D oug Sanders is best known for his short swing and colorful wardrobe, but lost in all that is the fact that he was a very talented shot-maker and a player skilled enough to win nineteen times on the PGA Tour, including the 1956 Canadian Open, which he won while still an amateur. He also finished second in two British Opens, both times to Jack Nicklaus. He also finished second in the 1961 U.S. Open and tied for second in the 1959 PGA Championship. Throughout his career, the adjective "colorful" was inexorably linked to his name, and surely no other word was quite as fitting.

Doug Sanders combined a healthy belief in his own skills and a gambler's eye for the odds. He was never afraid to take a gamble and was particularly happy to play with his own money on the line.

In the 1966 Bob Hope Desert Classic, Sanders found himself heading toward a playoff with Arnold Palmer, who would win the tournament five times, including in 1973, which was his last tour victory.

Facing the ultracompetitive Palmer in a playoff was never an easy task, but it was especially daunting in the desert, where he could comfortably unleash his considerable power without being overly concerned about things like deep rough or penal hazards. Standing on the first tee, Sanders knew he had to nick Palmer before they reached a par-5, where Palmer's length would give him a huge edge over Sanders.

Suddenly, Sanders had a brainstorm: he would turn the odds in his favor by turning up the pressure on Palmer.

"Arnie, let's play winner-take-all," Sanders said, loud enough so he could be heard by the gallery. "What do you say?"

Now it's worth noting that in those days players involved in playoffs would occasionally agree to split the combined first- and second-place purses, although it was rarely mentioned or reported upon.

Palmer looked at Sanders as though his opponent had lost his mind, and after thinking it over, he declined the offer. It was just as well, because on the first hole of their playoff, Sanders ripped a 7-iron to within eighteen feet of the hole and made the putt for birdie and the win.

...

One year Sanders traveled to Scotland for the British Open and decided to stay around and play some of the venerable old courses. When playing the most venerable of them all—the Old Course at St. Andrews—he came to the home hole. His drive landed just short of the large grassy hollow in front of the green known as the "Valley of Sin."

As Sanders approached his ball, one of his playing companions—a Scot—commented that it was sad that American golfers had never mastered the pitch and run, which is a staple of golf in Scotland because of the windy conditions and the firm links turf.

While that may have been true, it wasn't true when it came to Sanders, who was a genius with that shot. He suggested a small wager and then emptied all the balls from his bag. He hit each ball with a different club, and the worst shot came to rest just a few feet from the hole.

GENE SARAZEN

Anyone who doubts just how remarkable Gene Sarazen was in his prime needs to be reminded that he was the first player to win all four modern Grand Slam titles—the U.S. and British Opens, the Masters and the PGA Championship.

Sarazen was a fierce competitor, even late in his playing days.

"Once, when Gene was in his seventies, he and I played two tour pros who were down in Marco Island," recalled Ken Venturi, the 1964 U.S. Open champion and longtime golf commentator for CBS Sports. "I played pretty well, but Gene really played beautifully. We beat the kids and then went in and had lunch. When they got up to leave, Gene thanked them for the game.

" 'Good luck, fellas,' Gene said. 'Come back when you can play a little better.' "

...

In what has to be one of the all-time weirdest golf matches, Gene Sarazen—who at the time was the head professional at Briarcliff Manor near New York City—played a nine-hole match against a bait caster. The rules were simple: Sarazen would have to hole out on every hole, and the bait caster would have to land his lead weight inside a thirty-inch circle that had been painted on each green.

In what must have surely been one of his most embarrassing losses, Sarazen was clipped, 4 and 3.

SHELL'S WONDERFUL
WORLD OF GOLF

Shell's Wonderful World of Golf was one of the earliest—and easily the best—of the made-for-television golf shows. It featured the best golfers in the world playing on some of the finest courses in the world.

The show's producer and director was a New York advertising man named Fred Raphael who didn't know much about golf but knew how to produce great television. He also had a wealth of great stories.

"I stopped into a bar near my office one afternoon and a match was on the television behind the bar," Raphael recalled. "I said to the bartender, 'I bet you Snead wins.' He asked me how I knew and I told him I'd produced the show. Every week he'd ask me who won that week's match. I thought he was just being friendly. As it turns out, he was making a fortune betting on the matches."

VIJAY SINGH

Vijay Singh's rise to become the world's top-ranked golfer in 2004 is one of the most unlikely—and inspiring—stories in golf history.

Singh was born and raised in Fiji, one of the last places on earth anyone would expect to produce a world-class golfer, let alone one of the best players on the planet.

After turning pro, Singh played in tournaments in every corner of the globe before joining the PGA Tour and quickly establishing himself as one of the hardest-working players in the game—a work ethic that has paid off magnificently.

In the early years of his career, he and his wife, Ardena, watched their money closely, since there wasn't much of it to watch in those days. To supplement his tournament winnings, Singh would occasionally hold down club jobs or get involved in betting games. On one occasion, in Borneo, one such game turned out handsomely—but it was close to being a disaster.

"I was making about $600 a month plus my lessons working at a club job," Singh recalled. "I got into a match for about $800 and all I had was about the equivalent of three American dollars with me. It came down to the final hole—a par-five—and I hit my drive out-of-bounds. Fortunately, I made an eagle with my second ball and my opponent hit into the water twice. I'll tell you, that was a lot of pressure—much different from the pressure of trying to win a tour event. That day, I was wondering if I'd get out of there alive if I lost."

AL SMITH

Al Smith, the popular Democrat who served as governor of New York and was the first Roman Catholic to run for president of the United States, loved golf, even if he wasn't particularly good at the game.

If he was in a tight match, he would build little mounds of sand and then tee up his ball in the fairway. One day his opponent asked him how he could do that under the rules of golf.

"First, dear boy, I can do it because the sand is part of the golf course," Smith explained. "And second, I can do it because I'm the governor of the great state of New York."

WALKER B. SMITH

Walker B. Smith was a society swell who played a lot of golf at the best clubs in the metropolitan New York area in the early part of the twentieth century. Smith was a good player and particularly skilled at match play. But skill or no skill, he had a stunt that he often pulled on unsuspecting opponents that was sure to unnerve them.

If it was the first time he met his opponent(s), he would come to the first tee and announce that "golf requires two things: courage and the ability to keep your eye on the ball."

"This supplies the courage," he would say, taking a swallow of whiskey from the silver flask he always carried. Then he would pull out one of the spare glass eyes he carried in his bag and place it near his golf ball. "And that's how I keep my eye on the ball."

SAM SNEAD

It is said that one mark of greatness is when a person doesn't remind you of anyone else. By that measure alone, Sam Snead was a great man. Surely there has never been anyone like him—before or since his death a few years ago.

People often said that Sam hustled people, which is absurd. He was so good, he didn't need to hustle anyone, and most people were so nervous just playing with Sam that they couldn't play dead, let alone play well enough to beat him.

I was fortunate enough to play a lot of golf with Sam, either at The Homestead or at Pine Tree, where he played in the winter.

One day we were having lunch after a round at Pine Tree when an old friend from Sam's days in the Navy

during World War II joined us. The two soon began trading stories.

"People say Sam was a great player, but unless you played against him in his prime, you have no idea how great he really was," the man said. "We were stationed in San Diego and played a lot of golf. I was a plus-two and a buddy of mine was a scratch player. We'd play our best ball against Sam, no strokes, and we hardly ever beat him."

...

One day Sam was playing a practice round at the Masters with Tom Kite and Bobby Cole, a promising young player from South Africa. On the par-5 thirteenth hole, Sam hit a perfect drive, bending it around the corner into the fairway. As Cole prepared to hit his drive, Sam inserted the needle.

"You know, Bobby, when I was your age we'd just drive the ball right up over the top of those trees," Sam said.

Cole shifted his aim slightly to the left and blistered his tee shot. The ball screamed off the clubface, rising steadily until it crashed into the pines, rattled around, and fell into Rae's Creek.

"Of course, when I was your age those trees were a hell of a lot shorter," said Sam, chuckling as he walked off the tee.

...

"I always wanted to have a little something riding on a match, just to hold my attention," Sam often said. "If I didn't have a bet to play for, I'd rather play tiddledy-winks. It didn't have to be much, but it had to be something worth playing for.

"I pretty much enjoyed big-money matches but some were a little scary," Sam continued. "One time Mr. Icely, the head of Wilson Sporting Goods, wanted me to go to Cuba to play in a match for a friend of his. This guy had a big bet with a millionaire named Sanchez. This Sanchez character was willing to bet a ton that no one could beat his club pro, Rufino Gonzales, on his home course. I didn't want to go, but Mr. Icely insisted and he signed my checks, so off I went.

"I got down there and played a practice round with Rufino. I shot a 65 and while Rufino was a good driver and putter, I knew I'd beat him because I could reach every par-five in two and he couldn't reach a one of them.

"We got to the first tee the next day and there are these real mean-looking guys in the gallery. Rufino told me that Batista, the dictator, had bet heavily on him, and his security men were there to make sure there was no funny business. On top of that, Rufino told me there were so many side bets out there that the pot was over $100,000. I was in there for $250, but that was the least of my worries.

"I shot 69-68 and poor Rufino shot a couple of 72s. As we were walking back to the clubhouse, I started getting real nervous, because Batista's boys were closing in on us. I collected my winnings and hightailed it back to Florida, where Mr. Icely asked how I'd done.

"Just fine, Mr. Icely," I said. "But if it's all the same to you, next time you set up a match like that, send Jimmy Demaret. He likes to travel and he'd make a lot prettier corpse than I would."

...

One of Sam's best friends on tour was Bob Goalby, the 1968 Masters champion. They often played practice rounds together, as was the case at The Commemorative, a Champions Tour event run by *Golf Digest* at Newport Country Club in Rhode Island.

On this day, Sam and Chandler Harper agreed to play Goalby and Dow Finsterwald. As they arrived on the first tee, Harper complained about a sore back and Sam had to help his old friend tie his shoes.

"Now, look here, fellas," Sam said. "Chandler's in bad shape. He needs to get a little weight here. Give him a couple a side and we can have a game."

Goalby and Finsterwald agreed. Sam made seven birdies, Chandler made six, and to no one's surprise, they won easily.

"Here, you cheating SOB," Goalby said good-naturedly as he paid Sam.

"Cheating?" Sam protested. "How was I supposed to know old Chandler would make such a quick recovery?"

…

When Snead came out on tour in 1937 he was a virtual unknown, which isn't surprising since he had rarely left the confines of his hometown, Hot Springs, Virginia.

At one of the first tournaments he entered, whom should he run into but Dutch Harrison and Bob Hamilton, two gentlemen who loved nothing more than finding a nice young man and inviting him to join them for a practice round—with a little something on the line just to make it interesting, of course.

"I wasn't much on gambling and I didn't have much spare money, but I wanted to be one of the guys, so I went along," Snead frequently recalled over the years. "I got up on that first tee and hit the first two balls into the boonies. They were looking at each other trying to figure out where this hayseed came from. Well, after a while I settled down and started beating them pretty good. That's when Dutch tried to give me the needle.

" 'Young man, you've got a fine swing but we've got to do something about that grip of yours,' Dutch said. 'That hook grip will kill you out here, won't it, Bob?'

"I may have been wet behind the ears, but I had been around enough to know what he was trying to do," Sam said. "I thanked him very much and ignored him. I just played my own game and by the time we finished, I had won a little money from both of them. I thanked them for the game and asked if they wanted to play the next day.

" 'Sonny, you work your side of the street and we'll work ours,' Dutch said."

...

Early in his career, Sam used to drive from tournament to tournament with Johnny Bulla. The two became great friends and for a time—a short time, as it turned out—they had a standing bet that whoever had the best finish that week would win $5 from the other man.

"We were playing the Los Angeles Open and I had a pretty good finish," Bulla remembered. "I went out to watch Sambo play the eighteenth hole. He hit a good drive and I told him, 'Jackson, that sure looks like a six-iron to me.' He just looked at me, said 'Uh-huh,' and hit the prettiest little seven-iron in there that you've ever seen.

" 'You forced it,' I told him.

" 'Pay up,' Sam said.

"The next week he beat me again and I told him, 'Sambo, the game's off.' "

...

One year Sam and Jerry Barber were playing a match against Arnold Palmer and Dow Finsterwald during a practice round in Las Vegas. Everything went along just fine until the seventh hole.

"I had this kid caddying for me who was just a bag

carrier," Snead recalled. "He was a nice kid but he didn't know anything about golf. We all hit our drives on number seven and when we reached the fairway, the boy is cleaning off my ball with a towel.

"Arnold asked the kid what he was doing.

" 'Mr. Snead told me I had to keep his ball clean on every hole,' he said.

" 'Well, at least wait until we reach the green,' Palmer said."

...

Billy Farrell, whose father, Johnny, beat Bobby Jones in a playoff to win the 1928 U.S. Open, was the longtime head professional at The Stanwich Club in Greenwich, Connecticut. He also played the tour for many years. He was a close friend of Sam Snead's, and they played many practice rounds together. One day, they invited a young player named Raymond Floyd to join them.

"Raymond had a lot of confidence, even back then," Billy recalled. "He wouldn't back down from anyone and he wasn't afraid to put his own money out there. We arranged the bet and the three of us went off. Sam didn't play very well on the front nine and when we made the turn he wanted to raise the bets so he had a chance to get his money back. I told him I'd seen that act before and I'd just stick with the original bet. Raymond wanted all of Sam he could get—and that's just about what he got. Sam shot a 28 on the back and just killed Raymond. He beat him every way possible. It was a good lesson for the young man."

...

Legend has it that Snead learned to play golf by carving a branch of an old swamp maple into the shape of a golf club and hitting stones—or cow chips—around a pasture. Like most stories about Sam, there is an element of truth to it, but like the stories about Sam burying his money in tomato cans around his house, it tends to improve with age.

At any rate, one day a rich guy staying at The Greenbrier challenged Sam, saying he didn't believe a word of the story.

"I bet him I could go out and carve a club out of a tree limb and break 80 with just that club and a putter," Sam said. "He jumped on that bet like a dog on a bone. It was the easiest money I ever made."

...

Another legend that grew up around Sam was that he was miserly. That simply wasn't true. He could be generous to a fault—he just didn't want any publicity. That isn't to say, however, that he and his money were ever foolishly parted.

Sam's allure was something like that of the fastest gun in the Old West. People always wanted to challenge him. And since he was going to be spending four or so hours of his valuable time on the job, he figured he might as well have a little money riding on it.

Sam was a genius at figuring the odds, but even given his enormous talent, he occasionally lost. On one occasion he played poorly and, after the match, handed the man a $20 bill and shook his hand.

"Sam," the man said. "Do me a favor and autograph it for me."

"What for?" Sam asked.

"I want to frame it and hang it on my office wall," he said. "That way I'll have proof I won. Otherwise, no one will ever believe me."

"Here, give me that $20 back," Sam said. "I'll write you a check."

...

One year a sportswriter in Los Angeles bet Snead $1,000 that he couldn't take eighteen putts or less for eighteen holes. Sam labored over this for about a nanosecond and accepted the bet. He went out and deliberately missed every green on the front nine, pitching up and taking one putt on each green except one, where he chipped in. After nine holes, the writer had seen enough and offered to settle with Sam for $500—which Sam happily accepted.

...

Snead arrived at St. Andrews for the 1946 British Open and it is safe to say the Old Course was unlike anything he had ever experienced in championship golf. So, for that matter, were the caddies.

"I was playing a practice round with some of the fellas and we had a few quid on the line," Sam recalled. "We got to this one green and my caddie pointed to a spot and said it was where the hole would be cut in the final round.

" 'How do you know?' I asked him, thinking he might have some inside information.

" 'Because that's where it's been cut for the last fifty years,' he said."

And that's where it was in 1946 as well.

...

It's safe to say that during his long life, Sam Snead saw every variety of golfer, from the greatest champions to the worst beaters in history. One player was so bad, however, that he carved a special niche in Sam's memory.

"These guys lined up a match with me, and my partner was a nice enough old bird, but he was the worst golfer I think I've ever seen," Snead said. "He was just as nervous as could be, and I tried to calm him down, but it just wasn't taking. He drove it out-of-bounds on the first hole, and then whiffed twice on the second. I think he picked up on every hole and he was just having a rotten time. I kept encouraging him, but he was pretty much a basket case. Then, we came to a short par-four and his drive not only hit the fairway, but it also hit a sprinkler head. By the time it stopped rolling, he was only about fifty yards from the green, and since he was getting a stroke a hole, I thought he might make a par for birdie and settle down. Well, he sort of topped and shanked his second shot—which is pretty hard to do if you think about it—but the ball scurried up onto the green a few feet from the hole. I figured we were in like Flynn, but he hit his first putt twenty feet past the hole and his second put ran about that far past the cup again. After that, he asked me if he could just pick up, and I told him that was fine with me."

...

Edward, Duke of Windsor, who abdicated the British throne so he could marry Mrs. Wallis Simpson—clearly one of the weirdest trade-offs in history—was a passionate if not-very-talented golfer. Still, he loved hobnobbing with the top players. When he learned that he would be in Palm Beach at the same time Sam Snead would be in the area, he asked if a game could be arranged.

Days after their match, the duke contacted Fred Corcoran, Snead's longtime friend and agent, and asked if the duke could send Sam a check to settle their wager (a practice he generally disavowed, as mentioned above, since he believed that the honor of playing with someone as princely as him was a far greater reward than mere money). Corcoran, always the diplomat, assured the duke that Sam would much rather have an autographed photo. When the photo arrived, Sam quickly let Corcoran know what he thought.

"Next time," Sam said, "we'll take the check."

...

Most of the time, the bets on Snead's matches were for nominal amounts, and for most people, just being able to say they played with Sam was worth whatever they could afford to bet. This was obviously the case of the two men in this story.

"One day these two fellas showed up at the course where I used to play during the winter down in Boca Raton," Sam recalled. "They wanted to play for a little money, so we went at it. They were pretty good amateurs, but I got them for about $50 in the morning round. They raised the stakes in the afternoon, and by the time we got finished with all the presses and side bets, I had won about $700. They asked if we could play the next day and we went at it all over again. I was playing really good and the matches were all close and they were good guys, so we decided to play every day for the rest of the week. We played a few of the courses in the area just to make it interesting and I set four course records. The worst round I shot was a 67. I won about $10,000 for the week, but they were pretty well off and we shook hands and parted as the best of friends."

...

Sam Snead grew up in Hot Springs, Virginia, in the shadow of The Homestead, the elegant old society hotel nestled in the mountains. While he was affiliated with the hotel during his career, he also had a long affiliation with the equally splendid Greenbrier hotel in nearby White Sulphur Springs, West Virginia.

When Sam was at the Greenbrier, he would play golf almost daily with guests, and usually with a little something on the line. Sam's course of choice was the "Old White," which he knew like the back of his hand.

One of the curious aspects of the course is the sixteenth hole, which has two greens. Playing to the green on the right, the hole plays 394 yards. Playing to the green on the left adds twenty yards and also brings water into play.

Sam always decided which green they'd play to. If he was ahead in the match, they'd play to the green on the right. If, by some fluke, he was trailing, they'd play to the other green, since the added length gave him an edge and his opponents would be just about ready to choke at that point in the proceedings and were as likely as not to hit into the hazard.

...

When Tom Kite was about to begin his PGA Tour career, he was given a very good piece of advice by his longtime teacher, the legendary Harvey Penick: if you have an opportunity to play practice rounds with Sam Snead, jump at the chance.

"Sam was still fairly active on tour in the early 1970s," recalled Kite. "The first chance I had, I introduced myself and asked if I could join him for a practice round. He agreed and, of course, we played for a little something, just to make it interesting for Sam. He wouldn't give you lessons in the usual sense, but you could learn so much just from watching him. After I played with him a few times, I went back home to Austin and asked Mr. Penick if he thought it was possible for me to learn all the shots Sam had and hit them under pressure. I was disappointed when he said probably not, but he was right."

...

Sam enjoyed playing matches against the young players on tour. He always felt it helped keep his game sharp.

On one occasion, he was playing some kid who kept referring to him as "Mr. Snead."

"Junior," he said. "Let me give you a piece of advice: don't ever call someone you're trying to beat 'Mister.' "

LEFTY STACKHOUSE

Lefty Stackhouse was one of the great characters in the early days of the tour. He was a good player despite a temper that was legendary.

One day he was recruited to play in an exhibition match to raise money for war bonds. The match was in Knoxville, and Tennessee's greatest legend, World War I hero Sergeant Alvin York, was on hand.

Stackhouse was easily the best player in the field. He was guaranteed a fee just for showing up, plus he had a side bet going with one of his playing partners, and he soon had the match well under control.

The weather was hot and humid, and at the turn, Stackhouse put bottles of Coca-Cola spiked with rum in his bag. Lefty happily drank his way through the back nine and it wasn't long before the heat and the alcohol began to take their toll. On one of the closing holes, Lefty bent over to read the line of his putt (never mind that by this point he could barely see his ball) and passed out.

"That poor man exhausted himself," said Sergeant York. "I had no idea that golf was such a strenuous game."

T. SUFFERN TAILER

Tommy Tailer combined charm, good looks, and a potent golf game, and he became something of a legend in metropolitan New York golf circles for his willingness to play high-stakes matches.

"I first met Tommy in the 1930s," recalled Sam Snead. "I had just come out of Hot Springs, and not many people in the New York area had heard of me. Some of his friends had, though, and they brought me up to Long Island to play a $500 nassau against Tommy. Tommy was hot to trot, and since I was playing with his friends' money, I was ready to get at it. Tommy threw me a stymie on the ninth hole and won the front side, but I won the back and the match and left town with a nice piece of change.

"About a year later another hotshot New York amateur

named Bunny Bacon arranged a match between us, Tommy, and a Dr. Hochschield. The match was for $5,000 and I was guaranteed $300 plus expenses, win or lose, and an extra $300 if Bunny and I won. On top of that, Bunny had laid off another $2,000 side bet with the doctor and flashed me a look at the $10,000 he was carrying. That kind of got my attention and tightened me up a bit. I topped my tee shot and second shot on the first hole, and that brought Bunny a-running.

" 'Sam,' he asked, 'Tommy didn't get to you, did he?'

"I showed him with my clubs. Bunny and the doctor played awful, but Tommy and I went right to the hilt. I had him dormie four, but he birdied fifteen and sixteen. I eagled seventeen to finally close them out. I took my $600 and Bunny collected seven grand. After the match, Tommy and I shook hands and he said, 'Sam, I never want to see you again.' "

...

"There was a time when Tommy's betting got him in a hole and he had to take a job selling a new board game at one of the big New York department stores," Sam Snead remembered. "You had to roll a little marble down a piece of wood with a bunch of holes drilled in it. It was hard to do, but Tommy was great at it because he had such wonderful hand-eye coordination. He was a natural salesman and made a lot of money in a hurry. As soon as he did, he headed to Florida where he had some matches lined up. One of them was with two hustlers at Indian Creek, where Tommy got clipped for $2,000.

"I never saw Tommy get mad, but I heard he was pretty hot when he came off the course," Sam continued. "But when he got in the locker room, what did he see but one of those board games.

" 'My, my, what's this?' he asked, and before you knew it, he had those old boys on the line. He tanked his first couple of tries, just to build up the pot, then ran the table on them. He just cleaned them out completely. They didn't know what hit them."

TEMPER, TEMPER

B obby Jones once famously observed that, on occasion, golf is a game that cannot be suffered with a club in your hands. In other words, while patience is a virtue, golfers sometimes find it exceedingly difficult to be virtuous when facing the onslaught of outrageous fortune. Take this story about two old friends who always partnered in their club's team championship.

They managed to reach the finals—the best they had ever done—and not only was the championship on the line, but a fair amount of money in the club's calcutta pool as well.

The match was tight, but it turned when they reached the seventeenth hole. With his partner out of the hole, the other player faced a long second shot to the green.

"What should I hit?" he asked his partner.

"Hit your four-wood," his partner said. "It's your favorite club."

"I don't have a four-wood," he said. "I must have left it in my locker."

Instead of his trusty 4-wood, he tried to reach the green with a long iron, with the predictable results. They went on to lose the hole and the match.

The following weekend, the two men showed up at the course for their usual weekend game. When they walked into the pro shop, one of the assistant pros came out of the workshop holding a 4-wood.

"Good news!" he said. "We found your club. It fell out of a tree on the sixteenth hole yesterday. Almost hit one of the greenskeepers on the head."

TITANIC THOMPSON

I t is quite possible that in the annals of golf, no one even approached Titanic Thompson as a hustler. He was an outstanding player, but he realized early on that—given the paltry purses pros played for in those days—he could make a better living through hustling.

"Titanic once asked me if I thought he could beat anyone playing left-handed if he got nine and a half strokes a round," recalled Paul Runyan, the two-time winner of the PGA Championship. "I told him I thought that was quite possible. He practiced very hard, then went to Dallas, where he had a couple of pigeons lined up. He played several rounds in the 80s just to set the trap, and then offered to play their best ball. He won $5,500 and then, being the sport that he was, offered them a chance to play the next day, double-or-nothing. He wound up winning over $20,000.

"That night, as he was leaving a casino, a caddie tried to rob him. Titanic shot him with the .45 he always carried and killed him instantly. I should add that it wasn't a fluke. Ti was a brilliant shot."

...

Back in the 1950s, Titanic heard about a kid in Ohio who was supposed to be a terrific player but was largely unknown. His nickname was "Stick" and he was said to be good enough to give another, somewhat more heralded junior named Jack Nicklaus a run for his money.

Thompson arranged for Stick to come to Texas—a testimonial to his salesmanship—so he could check out his game. After he saw Stick fire off a 66 on a course the first time he'd seen it, Thompson knew he had his man. He arranged for Stick to come to Indiana, where Thompson owned a farm that was adjacent to a golf course.

For days on end, Stick would drive a tractor around the fields adjacent to the course, feigning interest in the game that was being played on the holes that bordered the farm. Then, a week or so later, Thompson set the hook: when Stick saw Thompson come along, playing with the club's professional and two of its wealthier members, Stick jumped down from the tractor and sat atop the fence, for all intents and purposes enthralled by what he saw.

"Say, look at that boy over there," Thompson said, pointing to Stick. "I think he's interested in golf. He might make a good caddie."

By the end of the round, Thompson had convinced the pro to give Stick a few lessons. They must have been painful for the kid, having to produce a collection of whiffs, shanks, and foozles. Eventually—and right on Thompson's schedule—Stick began to make achingly slow progress.

Thompson was seemingly so impressed by the boy's progress and devotion to the game that he made a generous offer.

"I'd like to give him a taste of competition, just to see what he's made of," said Thompson. "I'll take him as a partner. You'll have to give him a lot of strokes, but we won't play for much."

They played the next day and Stick shot a fairly miraculous 100. With his strokes, and with Thompson playing just about as well as he needed to, he and Stick nearly broke even.

A rematch was arranged, with Stick receiving fewer strokes—owing to his astonishing improvement—and, at a significantly higher bet, the four players set out.

Imagine the marks' surprise when Stick shot a 66.

...

One day Titanic Thompson—who was ambidextrous—offered to play Lee Trevino if Trevino would use Titanic's left-handed clubs.

Trevino agreed, and on the first hole of their match, he hit a 3-wood into the fairway, a 5-iron onto the green and two-putted for a par that was good enough to win the hole.

Thompson had seen enough.

"Here," he said, paying Trevino. "You're a freak."

...

One story has it that Titanic Thompson earned his nickname by dressing as a woman and escaping from the *Titanic*, just as the ocean liner was about to sink. A more likely explanation is that he was running the table during a pool match when someone suggested he should be called Titanic because he was "sinking everybody" in the pool hall.

One of Titanic's favorite hustles was to show up at a club, find a few local swells who liked to gamble, and manage to give them a spirited match playing right-handed. Depending on his mood, he might let them win just enough to keep them interested. Then he would bait the trap.

"I'm not playing worth a damn," he'd say. "I'd be better off playing left-handed."

Usually, that was all it took. He'd get the bets up to a nice, healthy level, and then clean their clocks.

...

Thompson had phenomenal hand-eye coordination. For example, he had an uncanny ability to flip playing cards into a hat. He was also very good at tossing silver dollars into a hole, a trick he performed regularly—and profitably—at Tenison Park Golf Course in Dallas. It worked something like this . . .

Ti would hang around the putting green, casually

flicking coins toward a hole, making sure not to get many—if any—actually into the hole. Once people gathered to watch, he'd go into his act.

"I bet you $100 I could make one out of three," he'd say. Few people were gullible enough to take that bet.

"I could possibly even make two out of three," he'd continue, and while that might occasionally lure some fool, most held out.

"I'm not sure, but if I had to, I might get lucky and make three out of three," he'd add.

At that point someone was sure to take the bet, and the next sounds you'd hear would be the "clink, clink, clink" of three silver dollars hitting the metal liner of the cup.

...

One day Titanic was playing golf with a man who trained prize-winning bird dogs. The dog the man brought to the course that day was particularly well behaved. At one point during their round, Ti bet the man he could get the dog to bark in less than a minute. The man knew his dog and took the bet in a heartbeat, but what he didn't know was that Thompson had spotted a rabbit hiding in a small ditch about a hundred yards from the tee. No sooner had the man accepted the bet than Ti ripped a low, screaming drive that nearly hit the rabbit, sending him racing across the fairway—with the dog in close pursuit, barking madly.

...

One of Thompson's favorite hustles involved putting.

He would go out late in the day and stretch a garden hose across a green that had just been watered. He'd leave the hose on the green overnight and arrive early the next morning and remove it. After the green was cut, it would leave a trough that was virtually undetectable but allowed the ball to run straight into the hole.

Then he'd wait for a sucker to come along and bet him that he could make at least three of five putts from thirty feet.

It was a bet he never lost.

JIM THORPE

Jim Thorpe grew up in North Carolina next to the Roxboro Country Club, where his father, Elbert Sr., was the greens superintendent. The ninth of twelve children—several of whom became very good golfers— Jim was a good enough football player to earn a scholarship at Morgan State University. Unlike so many players who honed their golf games in college and top amateur competition, Thorpe polished his game playing money matches on the public courses around Washington, D.C., and Baltimore. He won three times on the PGA Tour and coming into the 2005 season had won thirteen events on the Champions Tour.

"The key to winning money at these public courses was to only play as good as you needed to play to win," Thorpe recalled. "If you went low too often, word would get around and either you wouldn't get any matches or you wouldn't get any matches you could win. If I had to shoot a 40 to win, that's what I'd shoot. If someone got hot and I had to shoot a 34, I could shoot that, too. The key was to get the odds in your favor before you even teed it up. Most times I had a match won before I even put a tee in the ground."

Most of Thorpe's early matches were played at a course called Clifton Park in Baltimore. He cut his teeth on $25 nassaus but soon set his eyes on higher stakes and took his action to East Potomac Golf Course in the District of Columbia.

"There were all sorts of characters over at East Potomac," Thorpe said. "There was this dude named Waldo who'd show up in pants that were three sizes too big and he'd have $20,000 in cash in each pocket. There were numbers runners, pimps—you name it. They'd come loaded with cash and no one would ever use his real name."

…

One of Thorpe's favorite stories concerns a character named Joe Pew.

"Joe Pew was a good player and he loved to gamble," said Thorpe. "His favorite bet was $500 a side and I knew if I could beat him, word would get around Baltimore and I could get into some big-stakes matches."

There was only one problem: Mr. Joe Pew was wise to the ways of the world and, before he'd tee it up, he wanted to see the money—and Jim Thorpe had exactly $104 to his name.

"I went to the bank and got a $50 bill and fifty-four ones. I rolled up the ones, put the $50 bill on the outside, and then wrapped an elastic band around them. When I got to the course, I flashed the roll at Joe but told him I couldn't show it to him because we were being watched."

The match proceeded beautifully. Thorpe won the front side and came to the eighteenth hole needing a halve to win $1,000. There was just one catch.

"Back in those days, I had three basic shots: a hook, a big hook, and a hook that would go from here to there and run forever," recalled Thorpe. "You had to drive through a chute of trees and there wasn't enough room out on the right side for me to start the ball. My drive hit a tree and bounced back toward the tee. Joe hit a good drive and was out there in the middle of the fairway. All I could do was knock my ball down the fairway, somewhere near the green. When Joe hit his approach three feet from the hole, I'm thinking, 'Good-bye money.' Now I've got a tough little pitching wedge and I'm choking my brains out. I skulled it and it took off. I figured I was dead, but it hits the flag going about a hundred miles an hour and drops straight down into the cup for a three. Joe about died on the spot. I took that money, said, 'Thank you very much for the game,' and got out of there as fast as I could."

...

Eventually, Thorpe was good enough to take his game out of town, which he did with some regularity and profitability.

"It was in the mid-1970s, and I was just starting out on tour and was struggling to get some financial backers," said Thorpe. "I just figured I had to do what I did best, which was find some big-money matches. Somebody set me up with a match against a guy I had never heard of in Detroit. I figured if he wasn't on tour and I had never heard of him, there wasn't any way he was going to beat me—and I was right.

"The first day we played at a place called Radrick Farms in Detroit and I whipped him pretty good," said Thorpe. "I mean, he couldn't play a lick that day. The next day we went to his home course, the Toledo Country Club. He played better, but I still beat him. In the end I won about $55,000 and, after I split it with my backers, I took home about $15,000, which went a long way in those days."

Of course, sometimes things didn't work out quite so well.

"I got set up in a match against this guy at Coffin Golf Club in Indianapolis," Thorpe recalled. "We were playing for $5,000. I shot a 33 on the front and he shot a 32. On the back nine we bet another $5,000. I shot another 33 and he shot another 32. I shook his hand, paid up, and told him, 'My man, you're the best.'"

…

When Jim Thorpe was trying to finance his early years on tour, he clearly struggled, but he never gave up hope—and with a little bit of luck, he finally made it.

"I was playing in a pro-am and they had a par-three that offered a new car if you made a hole-in-one," said

Thorpe. "I made one and asked one of the tournament officials what the car was worth. When I found out it was worth $8,000, I sold it on the spot, took the money, and headed to the qualifying school."

...

The lessons of his hustling days served Thorpe well once he made it on tour.

"I was playing in the Tucson tournament in 1985, when it was a match play tournament," said Thorpe. The tournament was played at match play from 1984 to 1986, and Thorpe won twice in that stretch. "I'm playing Dan Pohl and I've got him three-down and talking to himself pretty good. All of a sudden, he turns things around and the next thing I know, we're tied. We were playing the sixteenth hole and we both chipped to about two feet from the hole. Dan gave me my putt and I was getting ready to concede his when my caddie, Herman Mitchell, told me to make him putt it. Dan was looking at me, waiting for me to give him the putt, and when I didn't I think it kind of rattled him a little bit. He missed his putt and I went on to win. That was just my game, hitting shots and getting into the other guy's head."

JOE TORRE

One day New York Yankees manager Joe Torre was playing golf with former pitchers Ron Guidry and Mel Stottlemyre and one of his favorite coaches, Don Zimmer.

Zimmer, who had enjoyed success both as a player and as a manager with the Boston Red Sox and the Chicago Cubs, made a hole-in-one. Usually this is a cause for celebration, but not in this case, since Zimmer realized that much of the Yankee organization was at the course that day and the cost of drinks could easily run to $300 or $400—all at his expense.

That could help explain why, when they got to the next hole, Zimmer teed up the same ball he'd made the ace with—and promptly knocked it in the water.

"It was his first hole-in-one and he claimed he didn't

know he was supposed to keep the ball," said Torre. "I think he wanted it to be where most of his golf balls eventually wound up—someplace safe where they'd never be found again."

LEE TREVINO

Lee Trevino grew up dirt-poor in Dallas and went on to become one of the game's greatest champions. He's also a great storyteller.

"I played a lot on a public course in Dallas called Tenison Park," Trevino said. "It was so tough out there that people would skip an entire stretch of holes away from the clubhouse for fear of getting robbed.

"One day these two guys are out on one of those holes and the bets are flying fast and furious," Trevino continued. "One guy goes down $1,000 just as two guys with guns come out of the trees and hold them up.

" 'Here,' said the guy who was down $1,000, handing the cash to his opponent. 'We're even.' "

...

According to Trevino, Tenison Park was a betting golfer's paradise.

"There was a guy there named Dick Martin, who was probably the best player I ever saw until I saw Jack Nicklaus," Trevino said. "He just loved to come up with these crazy betting games. One was called the 'tunnel.' Everyone put up $25 and you went out to the farthest point of the course and you had to play your way back in. The tough part was playing through a narrow concrete tunnel. If you hit your ball over it you had to go back and try and play through it. It could take ten or fifteen shots to get through there. Another game was called 'trees,' where you had to pay the other guys for every tree you hit, and man, there were a lot of trees at Tenison Park. You could pay out some cash playing that game. There were all kinds of games out there. Another one was called 'Honest John,' where you had to pay a certain amount of money for every stroke you took. If you had a bad day, and the other guys played good, you could get killed."

...

When Jim Thorpe came out on tour in the mid-1970s,

Lee Trevino was one of the veteran players who took him under his wing.

One year Thorpe, Trevino, Andy Bean, and J. C. Snead were playing a practice round at Hilton Head and Thorpe learned a valuable—if costly—lesson.

"We came to the fourteenth hole, which is a good par-three over the water," said Thorpe. "I was thinking it was probably an eight-iron, but Trevino got up and hit a six-iron about eight feet from the hole. Now I know I'm at least one club longer than Lee, so I hit a seven. The ball was still rising when it went over the green. We're walking off the tee and Lee says to me, 'Man, don't ever look at what club I'm hitting. I've got so many shots you can never tell what I'm doing with the ball.'"

...

One year, during a practice round at the Masters, Lee Trevino bet one of his playing companions that he could skip his ball across the water on the par-3 sixteenth and make a par. The man took the bet in a heartbeat.

Trevino pulled a 1-iron from his bag and the other man watched as the ball skipped across the pond and bounced up on the green. Two putts later, Trevino had won the bet.

...

One of the most famous Lee Trevino stories involved the betting matches he used to play with a 32-ounce bottle of Dr Pepper. He was working at a driving range in Dallas at the time, and used to fool around hitting balls with the bottle, just to amuse himself.

There was a regular customer who used to come by to play Trevino. Naturally, Trevino could beat the guy like a drum, so one day he challenged the man to a different bet: Trevino would play the guy using just the Dr Pepper bottle. They'd bet on each hole, and if they tied a hole, it counted as a win for Trevino. Not surprisingly, Trevino owned him.

Soon word got around about the bet, and more people came from all around Dallas to challenge Trevino, who raked in the money.

After Trevino won the 1968 U.S. Open and became one of the game's most popular figures, one of his first endorsement contracts came from the company that made Dr Pepper.

...

No book of golf gambling stories would be complete without this classic tale about Lee Trevino and Raymond Floyd.

At the time, Floyd was in his early twenties and living the bachelor life in Dallas. He was already one of the bright young stars on the PGA Tour and had a reputation for being a player who wasn't afraid to put his own money on the line. At the same time, Trevino was working at a course named Horizon Hills out in west Texas. He was well known in Texas golf circles, but his reputation hadn't made it out of the state.

Some of the biggest gamblers in Dallas arranged for Floyd to come to Horizon Hills to play a series of high-stakes money matches against Trevino, who would be backed by some of the wealthy locals.

When Floyd arrived at the club, Trevino went and picked him up in a golf cart, then carried Floyd's clubs into the pro shop. Floyd asked Trevino who he was playing.

"Me," said Trevino.

"What do you do here?" Floyd asked, incredulously.

"Everything," said Trevino. "I'm the pro, the

shoeshine guy, the clubhouse manager, and I take care of the carts."

Floyd found one of his backers and told him he didn't need to look at the course before they played. Apparently—and logically—it didn't seem possible that this jack-of-all-trades could beat a tour pro.

Off they went, early in the afternoon, with a large gallery following them. Floyd shot a 67, which was fine except for the fact that Trevino shot a 65. Floyd asked if Trevino wanted to play another nine.

"I'd like to but I can't," said Trevino. "I've got to put the carts away and clean up the clubs. I've got a lot of work to do."

While Trevino busied himself around the clubhouse, Floyd and the rest of the guys played some cards, went dove hunting, and then headed across the border to Juárez, Mexico, for an evening's entertainment.

The next day they went out again, but this time with a larger gallery—and more money on the line. This time Floyd shot a 66—and Trevino shot a 65. Again, Floyd asked if Trevino wanted to go another nine. Again, Trevino begged off and went about his business. Floyd went and played cards.

On the third day, they went at it again. This time

Floyd won the front nine, but Trevino's backers pressed. On the back side Floyd shot a 31 and Trevino shot a 30.

After they finished, Floyd shook Trevino's hand.

"I've had enough," said Floyd. "I can find much easier games than this."

GENE TUNNEY

Unlike Joe Louis, Gene Tunney, another boxing heavyweight champion of the world, never harbored any illusions about his golf skills. And given this story from Paul Runyan, that was probably just as well.

"The Seminole Pro-Am used to be one of the premier events on the tour," recalled Runyan. "The club offered a good purse and, of course, there was a lot of betting on the different teams. One year I was paired with Gene Tunney. We got on the first tee and, as was my practice with my partners in team events, I shook his hand and told him I was going to play as hard as I possibly could. I told him I knew he was, too, and I told him there would be no apologies for poor shots or missed putts.

"His first drive went a full 310 yards and then he hit

his next shot within a few feet of the hole," said Runyan. "No one had even hinted that he could play like this. I was just thrilled to make his acquaintance and hadn't given a thought to winning. Just as I was beginning to think we might do very handsomely, he got over his putt and knocked it some twenty feet past the hole. At that point, I decided that I would enjoy his company but not worry too much about winning."

HARRY VARDON

Any list of the game's greatest champions has to include England's Harry Vardon, the winner of a record six British Opens and a U.S. Open. His exhibition tours of the United States (usually accompanied by fellow Englishman Ted Ray) are widely credited with helping to popularize the game in North America.

Although he suffered from failing health—most notably tuberculosis—he remained a force to be reckoned with in major championships into his fifties. In fact, he finished second to Ray in the 1920 U.S. Open at Inverness Club after missing a three-foot putt on the seventy-second hole.

After his loss, a member asked Vardon how a player of his magnitude could miss such a seemingly easy putt. Vardon—who didn't suffer fools gladly under the best of circumstances—bet the gentleman $100 that one week from that day, he could not sink the same putt Vardon had missed. And he could practice the putt to his heart's content.

The man agreed and the bet made the local papers all week. Much to the man's surprise, an enormous crowd gathered at Inverness, which was just what Vardon had anticipated. When the man's putt failed to even threaten the hole, Vardon collected $100 and many times more than that in satisfaction.

...

In Harry Vardon's time, there were still plenty of good amateurs who could compete with the top professionals of the day. Still, when Vardon was at his best, he was very nearly unbeatable—by pros and amateurs alike.

In 1899, Vardon came to America for one of his popular and lucrative exhibition tours. In the course of his visit, a much-publicized match was arranged between Vardon and two of the top amateurs in the United States: H. M. Harriman, the reigning U.S. Amateur champion, and Findlay S. Douglas, who had won the championship the previous year and was runner-up to Harriman in his defense of the title.

It wasn't even close.

Vardon played their best ball and won 9 and 8.

KEN VENTURI

K en Venturi's victory in the 1964 U.S. Open is considered one of the most heroic performances in the history of golf. Venturi had been one of the nation's top amateurs, almost winning the 1956 Masters before turning professional. He won fourteen PGA Tour events before his career was cut short by a series of injuries, but went on and enjoyed a long and successful career as the golf analyst for CBS Sports.

In 1956, Venturi was involved in what many people believe was the greatest money match of all time.

"I was playing in the Crosby and early in the week there was a cocktail party at George Coleman's house," Venturi recalled years later. "Eddie Lowery [who had caddied for Francis Ouimet in his 1913 U.S. Open victory and employed Venturi in his San Francisco car dealership] was there and he was telling Coleman about the match Harvie Ward and I had in the finals of the San Francisco City Championship [which Venturi won]. Eddie said he thought Harvie and I could beat any two players in the world—pros included.

"Well, one thing led to another," said Venturi, "and pretty soon Coleman said he'd take Byron Nelson and Ben Hogan and they agreed on a $50,000 bet."

The match was scheduled for the next morning at Cypress Point. To try and deter spectators, a bogus tee time was made at Pebble Beach, but by the time the four teed it up a large gallery had gathered anyway. If Venturi, who was only twenty-five, and Ward, who was thirty, were the least bit intimidated, it didn't show. (On reflection, they had reason to be confident. Ward was every bit Venturi's equal. He was the reigning U.S. Amateur champion and would successfully defend his title later in the year. He had also won the 1952 British Amateur, played on three Walker Cup teams, and finished fourth in the 1957 Masters.)

"We halved the first hole with pars and then the next eight holes were halved with birdies," Venturi remembered. "On ten, Ben holed a sand wedge to go one-up and then we halved the next three holes with birdies.

We halved fourteen with pars and fifteen, sixteen, and seventeen with birdies.

"On eighteen, I made an uphill twelve-footer for a birdie and that left it up to Ben, who had a real tough, right-to-left ten-footer to tie me on the hole and win the match," said Venturi. "Byron said, 'C'mon Ben, knock it in.' Ben said, 'Don't worry, I'm not going to let us get beat by a couple of amateurs.' "

He put it right in the middle of the hole.

For the record, Hogan shot a 63, Venturi shot a 65, and Nelson and Ward shot 67s. Hogan and Nelson were 17 under par. Between the four players there were twenty-seven birdies and an eagle.

"All four of us played about as well as we could play," Nelson said later.

For his part, Venturi put the match in a slightly different perspective.

"Harvie and I were best friends, and maybe this is being a little cocky, but we really believed we could take on the world," said Venturi. "Thinking back on it, that's pretty much what we did."

...

Ken Venturi was involved in a match with a player who was something of a stickler for the rules. On the thirteenth hole, Venturi's approach shot came to rest inches from the hole. Thinking the man would surely give him the putt, he swept it away from the hole and began to walk off the green.

"Ken, I didn't give you that putt," his opponent said. "Since we're playing strictly by the rules, I'm afraid you lost the hole."

Venturi was stunned.

"That means I'm three-down with five holes left," Venturi said. "Are you sure you want to win like that?"

"I'm sorry, Ken, but the rules are the rules," he said.

"You're positive you want to win like that?" repeated Venturi.

"I'm afraid so," the man said.

"Good," said Venturi. "You've got fifteen clubs in your bag. I win."

And with that, he and his caddie headed for the clubhouse.

TOM WATSON

By winning five British Opens, Tom Watson joined an elite group: only Harry Vardon won more—six—and only Peter Thomson and James Braid won as many.

Following his victory in the 1980 British Open at Muirfield, Watson and Ben Crenshaw and their wives were having dinner at the notoriously starchy club when a fan stopped by and gave Crenshaw—an avid collector—four hickory-shafted clubs and a handful of gutta-percha balls. The boys couldn't resist trying them, so after dinner they went out and played numbers ten and eighteen. They halved the tenth with fives and Watson won the eighteenth with a four.

As they were walking off the eighteenth green, the club's infamous secretary, Paddy Hammer, stalked out of the clubhouse and berated the two for trespassing on the hallowed turf of Muirfield without permission from a higher authority—him.

MIKE WEIR

When Mike Weir won the 2003 Masters, he became the first Canadian golfer to win at Augusta. In fact, he might well be the first Canadian to ever win one of the four major professional championships.

As a youngster, the left-handed Weir wondered if he should try to learn to play right-handed, as so many lefties have historically done, mostly due to the dearth of decent equipment for left-handers. Trying to make up his mind, he did a very logical thing: he wrote to the greatest player in the history of the game—Jack Nicklaus—and asked him what he thought. It is a measure of the man that Nicklaus wrote back a thoughtful letter, advising the kid to stick it out as a lefty. From that moment on (if he hadn't been before) Nicklaus was a hero in Weir's eyes.

As you can imagine, it was quite a thrill when he finally got a chance to play with Nicklaus during a practice round at Jack's tournament, The Memorial.

"It was Alejandro Larrazabal, who won the 2002 British Amateur, and me against Jack and his son, Gary," said Weir. "It was on a Wednesday and we knew that Jack would have to leave early because he hosted a ceremony in the afternoon. We got to the sixteenth hole and they were one-up. I hit it about twelve feet from the hole and Gary was fifteen feet away. When Gary missed his putt, Jack said, 'Well, at least we won one-up.' I knew he was trying to get into my head, so I said, 'Not yet.' I made my putt and we tied."

TOM WEISKOPF

Tom Weiskopf, whose career highlights include victories in the 1973 British Open and 1995 U.S. Senior Open, was an enormous talent who quite simply seemed to get bored with tournament golf and elected to focus his attention on his golf course design work, which has met with nearly universal praise. Weiskopf was one of the first in the long line of "Next Nicklauses," which is understandable since he followed Jack to Ohio State University and then out on tour. Being compared with Nicklaus was both a blessing and a curse, and while they've been friends over the years, they've also been rivals.

One year they were playing at Pebble Beach and on the par-5 eighteenth hole they both hit great drives. As Weiskopf prepared to hit his second shot, Nicklaus proposed a bet.

"Eagles for dinner?" Jack asked.

"Sure," said Weiskopf, and got into position over the ball. Suddenly, he backed off.

"Wait a minute, Jack," he said. "You've got your whole family here."

Finally, Weiskopf decided to go on with the bet, and he hit his second shot only to watch it come up short of the green, landing in the front bunker.

Nicklaus had 250 yards to the front of the green and hit a high, soft 1-iron that landed on the green and stopped quickly. A few minutes later, he made the putt for eagle—and Weiskopf knew that by the time dinner was over, he'd be a few hundred dollars poorer.

TIGER WOODS

One day, when Tiger Woods was just a kid, he came home with a pocket filled with change he had won in putting contests. His father took a dim view of gambling and told young Tiger he didn't want to see him come home with change that he won gambling.

A few days later, Tiger came home, but this time his pockets were filled with dollar bills. Earl was not pleased.

"Tiger, I told you I didn't want you to come home with money you won gambling," his father said, sternly.

"No, Pop," Tiger said. "You said I couldn't come home with *change* I won gambling."

...

Playing in a pro-am prior to the 2005 Bay Hill Invitational, Tiger Woods was paired with Indianapolis Colts quarterback Peyton Manning. For the first twelve holes, they enjoyed a lot of good-natured give-and-take, and Woods was generous with advice on Manning's game. But over the last six holes, things became a bit more serious.

"We had a bet going and he stopped giving me tips when he was trying to beat me," said Manning.

Woods showed just how ferocious a competitor he truly is on the eighteenth hole. With the bet on the line, he hit his approach shot on the demanding par-4 just eighteen inches from the hole for a tap-in birdie and the win.

After the round, Manning told reporters he thought Woods had the size and the hands to be a good receiver. Woods demurred.

"The first time I went over the middle I'd have my head taken off," he said.

...

When Woods was working with teaching professional Butch Harmon, the two enjoyed competing against each other in putting matches.

"If I won, Tiger would insist that we go another nine," said Harmon, the son of former Masters champion and legendary teacher Claude Harmon. "If he won that nine, we'd be done for the day. He used to beat me pretty regularly, unless we were at a major. Then, for some reason, I'd win.

"If I did win, he'd look at me with a funny look on his face and say, 'I don't understand how you can beat me. You're not any good.'"

BABE ZAHARIAS

By any standard, Babe Zaharias was one of America's greatest athletes. She won two gold medals and a silver medal in track and field in the 1932 Olympic Games and then, at the suggestion of famed sportswriter Grantland Rice, took up golf.

Even given her considerable athletic skills, her rise to excellence in the game was not only unusual, but very nearly unprecedented. Certainly other top athletes have made the transition to golf with some success, but none has gone on to dominate golf the way the Babe did. She won both the U.S. Women's Amateur and the Ladies British Open Amateur. Upon turning professional, she was one of the founding members of the Ladies Professional Golf Association and won forty-one LPGA titles, including three U.S. Women's Opens.

While her fellow players respected her ability, the truth is that her brash, hypercompetitive personality didn't always sit well with her contemporaries. They appreciated the attention she brought to the LPGA and to golf as a whole, but in many cases, their fondness pretty much ended there. A good example is this story about the Babe told by Peggy Kirk Bell, a fine player in her own right and one of the most respected teachers and beloved people in golf.

"As a rookie I was paired with Babe in a four-ball tournament," she said. "As you can imagine, I was deathly nervous. I met her in the locker room and told her I was going to try my hardest and I just hoped I could play well enough to help us win."

With other older, more experienced players looking on, Babe left no doubt about the inevitable outcome.

"Win!" she exclaimed. "Why, of course we'll win. I can beat any two of these girls on my own. You just tag along and have a good time."

. . .

In 1951, Zaharias issued a challenge to Leonard Crawley, one of England's most esteemed golf correspondents. She would bring a team of six of America's finest women golfers to Great Britain for a match against six of that nation's finest male amateurs, played from the championship tees at the famed Wentworth course.

While there wasn't much money on the line, there was national pride at stake, not to mention the fate of Crawley's magnificent red moustache, which he promised to shave off should the unthinkable occur and the men actually lose.

In the first match of the day, Crawley and Zaharias squared off, and, although he was a good player, he was no match for the Babe. She won 3 and 2 and the women won 6 1/2 to 2 1/2.

Happily, Zaharias took pity on Crawley, and his moustache was spared the razor.

A FEW GOLF GAMBLING TERMS YOU SHOULD KNOW

Arnies This is a bet that pays a player who makes par or better after missing the fairway from the tee. It is named after Arnold Palmer, who made a career out of salvaging pars from the rough. Occasionally the bet is doubled if a player makes par after missing both the fairway and the green.

barkies If your ball hits a tree and you're still able to make par, you win a barkie. Note that it must actually hit bark. Mere trifles, such as leaves, don't count. If you hit two trees on the same hole and still make par or better, the bet pays double.

best ball A form of team competition in which the best ball of a two-person team counts against the best ball of the other team. There is also a form of best-ball betting in which one player competes against the best ball of two or even three other players.

bingo bango bongo This is a bet in which three points are available on every hole. One point is awarded to the first player who hits the green. The second point goes to the player who is closest to the pin after all the approach shots have been hit. The third point is for the first ball in the hole. Note that putting is done according to which ball is farthest from the hole. In some variations, points are awarded for closest and next-closest to the hole following tee shots on par-3s. If only one player hits the green, he or she receives two points.

calcutta This is an auction in which people bid on the players or teams in a tournament before the tournament begins. The highest bid wins the team. Team owners can then sell shares in their team at any point in the tournament.

four ball This is a match pitting two teams of two players (a total of four balls being played, hence the name) against each other using best-ball scoring. All four players play their own ball throughout; at the end of each hole, the low score among the two partners on each team is that team's score. Four ball can be played as stroke play or match play and is one of the formats used in international team competitions.

Hogans This bet rewards a player who hits both the fairway and the green (in regulation) and goes on to make par. It is named in honor of Ben Hogan, who was a master of hitting fairways and greens.

low ball A simple bet in which, as the name suggests, a hole is won with the lowest score, generally in team play.

murphies A murphy is a side bet that can be invoked by a golfer who is chipping or pitching to the green. The player declaring "murphy" is betting that he or she can get up and down in two strokes. The amount of the bet must be decided before the round and players should agree if murphies are to be automatically accepted by the other players in the group, or if the other players get to decide whether to accept the bet on a case by case basis. And make sure everyone agrees on the area from which a murphy can be declared. Most groups rule out balls on the fringe.

nassau The nassau is one of the most popular golf bets. It's essentially three bets in one: low score on the front nine, low score on the back nine, and low eighteen-hole score all count as separate bets. In some formats, the bet on the eighteen-hole score is twice that of either nine. The most common form of nassau is the $2 nassau. The front nine is worth $2, the back nine is worth $2, and the eighteen-hole total is worth $2. A player or team sweeping all three wins $6.

press An extension of the original bet that, in effect, creates a new bet. This usually occurs when a player or team is two down. The team or player being offered the press is not required to accept it, but in some formats presses are automatic when one side is two down.

rabbit This side bet gets its name from the term used to describe a pacesetter. Here's how rabbit works: Prior to the start of the match, all players agree on the amount each hole is worth, say $1. The first player to have the low score on a hole captures the rabbit and $1 from each of the other players (if two players tie for low score, no one captures the rabbit). If someone other than the holder of the rabbit is the low scorer on the next hole, the rabbit changes hands and the new rabbit holder wins $1 from each of the other players. The rabbit is then won by the next player to get the low score on a hole. A player wins $1 from each of the other players on every hole until he gives up the rabbit.

round robin This game, sometimes called "Six, Six, and Six," is ideal for foursomes. Players rotate partners every six holes so that everyone eventually teams with every other player; each six-hole segment is a separate bet. If, at the end of eighteen holes, you've been on two winning sides and one losing side, you come out ahead.

scramble The scramble is one of the primary forms of tournament play for charity events or any other occasion when time is of the essence. A scramble is usually played with four-person teams but two-person scrambles are also played. Handicaps are often used in two-person scrambles, but not in four-person scrambles. Each player tees off on each hole and the best of the tee shots is selected; all players play their second shots from that spot. The best of the second shots is determined, then all play their third shots from that spot, and so on until the ball is holed.

skins In a skins game, each hole has a set value (usually in money or points). The player who wins the hole is said to win the "skin," and whatever that skin is worth. Skins games are often more dramatic than standard match play because holes are never halved. When players tie a hole, the value of that hole is added to the value of the next hole.

snake This is a side bet in which all players in a foursome agree on the value of the "snake" at the beginning of the round. The first player who three-putts keeps the snake until someone else three-putts. The player with the snake at the end of the round pays the other players in the foursome.

stableford In a stableford competition, golfers receive points based on their scores in relation to par—or some other fixed score—on each hole. The player finishing with the highest score wins. The point system used at the PGA Tour's International tournament, played annually at Castle Pines Golf Club in Colorado, is a good example of the stableford system. Players receive eight points for a double eagle, five points for an eagle, two points for a birdie, and zero points for a par; they lose one point for a bogey and three points for double bogey or worse. Variations of this point system can be found in the rules of golf.

Texas scramble In a Texas scramble, at least four drives of each member of the foursome must be used during the course of the round. In a regular scramble, a great driver might have his tee ball used on every hole. A Texas scramble eliminates that possibility and forces even the weakest driver on the team to get into the action.

trash Sometimes called "garbage," trash generally means any side bets such as greenies (hitting greens on par-3s), birdies, sandies (making par or better from a bunker), etc.

wolf Four players take turns being the "wolf." The player designated as the wolf decides whether to play the hole against the three other players in the group or chooses a partner immediately following that player's drive and then plays two-on-two. The side with the lowest better-ball score wins the hole. If it's a one-versus-three scenario, the wolf either wins or loses double.